Abbé Raynal

A Philosophical and Political History of the British Settlements and Trade in North America

Vol. I

Abbé Raynal

A Philosophical and Political History of the British Settlements and Trade in North America
Vol. I

ISBN/EAN: 9783743400443

Manufactured in Europe, USA, Canada, Australia, Japa

Cover: Foto ©ninafisch / pixelio.de

Manufactured and distributed by brebook publishing software (www.brebook.com)

Abbé Raynal

A Philosophical and Political History of the British Settlements and Trade in North America

A
Philosophical and Political
HISTORY
OF THE
British Settlements and Trade
IN
NORTH AMERICA.
Volume the First.

A
Philosophical and Political
HISTORY
OF THE
BRITISH
SETTLEMENTS AND TRADE
IN
NORTH AMERICA.

From the FRENCH *of Abbé* RAYNAL.

IN TWO VOLUMES.

VOL. I.

EDINBURGH:
Printed by C. MACFARQUHAR.
Sold by the BOOKSELLERS.
M.DCC.LXXVI.

CONTENTS

OF THE

FIRST VOLUME.

INTRODUCTION,   Page 9 to 47

1. First expeditions of the English in North America,   9
2. The continent of America is peopled by the religious wars that disturb England,   13
3. Parallel between the old and the new world,   25
4. Comparison between civilized people and savages,   37
5. In what state the English found North America, and what they have done there,   45

BOOK I.

BRITISH Colonies settled at HUDSON's BAY, NEWFOUNDLAND, NOVA SCOTIA, NEW ENGLAND, NEW YORK, and NEW JERSEY.

CHAP. I. Of HUDSON's BAY,   48 to 66
1. Climate. Customs of the inhabitants. Trade.   48
2. Whether there is a passage at Hudson's Bay leading to the East Indies,   59

CHAP. II. Of NEWFOUNDLAND, 66 to 86
1. Description,   66
2. Fisheries,   71

CHAP.

CONTENTS.

Chap. III. Of NOVA SCOTIA, 87 to 103

1. The French give up Nova Scotia to Britain, after having been a long time in possession of it themselves, 87
2. Manners of the French who remained subject to the British government in Nova Scotia, 93
3. Present state of Nova Scotia, 100

Chap. IV. Of NEW ENGLAND, 103 to 126.

1. Foundation, 103
2. Fanaticism occasions great calamities there, 108
3. Government, population, cultures, manufactures, trade, and navigation, 114

Chap. V. Of NEW YORK and NEW JERSEY, 126 to 141

1. New York, founded by the Dutch, passes into the hands of the English, 126
2. Flourishing state of New York. Causes of its prosperity. 131
3. In what manner New Jersey fell into the hands of the English. Its present state. 137

BOOK II.

British Colonies founded in Pensylvania, Maryland, Virginia, Carolina, Georgia, and Florida.

Chap. I. Of PENSYLVANIA, 142 to 178

1. The Quakers found Pensylvania. Manners of that sect. 142
2. Upon what principles Pensylvania was founded, 152
3. Extent, climate, and soil, of Pensylvania. Its prosperity. 157

Chap.

CHAP. II. Of VIRGINIA and MARYLAND,
                                    178 to 204
1. Wretched state of Virginia at its first settlement, 178
2. Administration of Virginia,   184
3. Maryland is detached from Virginia,   191
4. Virginia and Maryland cultivate the same productions,   194
5. Of the Tobacco-trade,   199

CHAP. III. Of CAROLINA,   205 to 221
1. Origin of Carolina,   205
2. System of religious and civil government established by Locke in Carolina,   ib
3. Climate and produce of Carolina,   211

CHAP. IV. Of GEORGIA,   221 to 230
1. Foundation of Georgia,   221
2. Impediments that have prevented the progress of Georgia,   225

CHAP. V. Of FLORIDA,   230 to 240
1. History. Its cession from the Spaniards to the British.   230
2. By what means Britain may render Florida useful to her,   237

A
Philosophical and Political
HISTORY
OF THE
BRITISH
Settlements and Trade in AMERICA.

INTRODUCTION.

1. *First Expeditions of the English in North-America.*

ENGLAND was only known in America by her piracies, which were often succesful and always brilliant, when Sir Walter Raleigh conceived a project to make his nation partake of the prodigious riches which for near a century past flowed from that hemisphere into ours. That great man, who was born for bold undertakings, cast his eye on the eastern coast of North-America. The talent he had for subduing the mind by representing all his proposals in a striking light, soon procured him associates, both at court and amongst the merchants. The company that was formed upon the allurements of his magnificent promises, obtained of government, in 1584, the absolute disposal of all the discoveries that should be made; and without any further encouragement, they fitted out two ships in April following, that anchored in Roanoak bay, which now makes a part of Carolina. Their commanders, worthy of the trust reposed in them, behaved with remarkable affability in a country where they wanted to settle their nation, and left the savages to make their own terms in the trade they proposed to open with them.

Every thing that these successful navigators reported on their return to Europe, concerning the temperature of the climate, the fertility of the soil, and the disposition of the inhabitants, encouraged the society to proceed. They accordingly sent seven ships the following spring, which landed a hundred and eight free men at Roanoak, for the purpose of commencing a settlement. Part of them were murdered by the savages, whom they had insulted; and the rest, having been so improvident as to neglect the culture of the land, were perishing with misery and hunger, when a deliverer came to their assistance.

This was Sir Francis Drake, so famous among seamen for being the next after Magellan who sailed round the globe. The abilities he had shewn in that grand expedition induced queen Elizabeth to make choice of him to humble Philip II. in that part of his domains which he made use of to disturb the peace of other nations. Few orders were ever more punctually executed. The English fleet seized upon St Jago, Carthagena, St Domingo, and several other important places; and took a great many rich ships. His instructions were, that, after these operations, he should proceed and offer his assistance to the colony at Roanoak. The wretched few, who had survived the numberless calamities that had befallen them, were in such despair, that they refused all assistance, and only begged he would convey them to their native country. The admiral complied with their request; and thus the expences that had been disbursed till that time were lost.

The associates, however, were not discouraged by this unforeseen event. From time to time they sent over a few colonists, who by the year 1589 amounted to a hundred and fifty persons of both sexes, under a regular government, and fully provided with all they wanted for their defence, and for the purposes of agriculture and commerce.

These beginnings raifed fome expectations, but they were loft in the difgrace of Ralegh, who fell a victim to the caprices of his own wild imagination. The colony, having loft its founder, was totally forgotten.

It had been thus neglected for twelve years, when Gofnold, one of the firft affociates, refolved to vifit it in 1602. His experience in navigation made him fufpect, that the right track had not been found out; and that, in fteering by the Canary and Caribbee iflands, the voyage had been made longer than it need have been by above a thoufand leagues. Thefe conjectures induced him to fteer away from the fouth, and to turn more weftward. The attempt fucceeded; but when he reached the American coaft, he found himfelf further north than any who had gone before. The region where he landed, fince included in New-England, afforded him plenty of beautiful furs, with which he failed back to England.

The fpeed and fuccefs of this undertaking made a ftrong impreffion upon the Englifh merchants. Several joined in 1606 to form a fettlement in the country that Gofnold had difcovered. Their example recalled to others the remembrance of Roanoak; and this gave rife to two charter companies. As the continent where they were to exercife their monopoly was then known in England only by the

the general name of Virginia, the one was called the South Virginia, and the other the North Virginia Company.

The firſt zeal ſoon abated, and there appeared to be more jealouſy than emulation between the two companies. Though they had been favoured with the firſt lottery that ever was drawn in England, their progreſs was ſo ſlow, that in 1614 there were not above four hundred perſons in both ſettlements. That ſort of competency which was ſufficient for the ſimplicity of the manners of the times, was then ſo general in England, that no one was tempted to go abroad by the proſpect of a fortune. It is a ſenſe of misfortune, ſtill more than the thirſt of riches, that gives men a diſlike to their native country. Nothing leſs than an extraordinary ferment could then have peopled even an excellent country. This was at length brought about by ſuperſtition, and excited by the colliſion of religious opinions.

2. *The continent of America is peopled by the religious wars that diſturb England.*

THE firſt prieſts of the Britons were the Druids, ſo famous in the annals of Gaul. To throw a myſterious veil upon the ceremonies of a ſavage worſhip, their rites were never performed but in dark receſſes, and generally

nerally in gloomy groves, where fear creates spectres and apparitions. Only a few persons were initiated into these mysteries, and intrusted with the sacred doctrines; and even these were not allowed to commit any thing to writing upon this important subject, left their secrets should fall into the hands of the profane vulgar. The altars of a formidable deity were stained with the blood of human victims, and enriched with the most precious spoils of war. Though the dread of the vengeance of heaven was the only guard of these treasures, they were always reverenced by avarice, which the druids had artfully repressed by the fundamental doctrine of the endless transmigration of the soul. The chief authority of government resided in the ministers of that terrible religion; because men are more powerfully and more lastingly swayed by opinion than by any other motive. The education of youth was in their hands; and the ascendency they assumed at that period remained through the rest of life. They took cognizance of all civil and criminal causes, and were as absolute in their decisions on state affairs as on the private differences between man and man. Whoever dared to resist their decrees, was not only excluded from all participation in the divine mysteries, but even from the society of men. It was accounted a crime and a reproach to hold any

converse

converse or to have any dealings with him; he was irrevocably deprived of the protection of the laws, and nothing but death could put an end to his miseries. The history of human superstitions affords no instance of any one so tyrannical as that of the druids. It was the only one that provoked the Romans to use severity, as none opposed the power of those conquerors with such violence as the druids.

That religion, however, had lost much of its influence, when it was totally banished by Christianity in the seventh century. The northern nations, that had successively invaded the southern provinces of Europe, had found there the seeds of that new religion, in the ruins of an empire that was falling on all sides. Whether it was owing to their indifference for their distant gods, or to their ignorance which was easily persuaded, they readily embraced a worship which from the multiplicity of its ceremonies could not but attract the notice of rude and savage men. The Saxons, who afterwards invaded England, followed their example, and adopted without difficulty a religion that secured their conquest by abolishing their old forms of worship.

The effects were such as might be expected from a religion, the original simplicity of which was at that time so much disfigured. Idle contemplations were soon substituted in lieu of active and social virtues; and a stupid veneration for unknown faints, to the worfhip of the Supreme Being. Miracles dazzled the eyes of men, and diverted them from attending to natural caufes. They were taught to believe that prayers and offerings would atone for the moft heinous crimes. Every fentiment of reafon was perverted, and every principle of morality corrupted.

Thofe who had been at leaft the promoters of this confufion, knew how to avail themfelves of it. The priefts obtained that refpect which was denied to kings; and their perfons became facred. The magiftrate had no infpection over their conduct, and they even evaded the watchfulnefs of the civil law. Their tribunal eluded and even fuperfeded all others. They found means to introduce religion into every queftion of law, and into all ftate affairs, and made themfelves umpires or judges in every caufe. When faith fpoke, every one liftened, in filent attention, to its inexplicable oracles. Such was the infatuation of thofe dark ages, that the fcandalous exceffes of the clergy did not weaken their authority.

This was owing to its being already founded on great riches. As foon as the priefts had taught that religion depended principally upon facrifices, and required firft of all that of fortune and earthly poffeffions, the nobility, who were fole proprietors of all eftates,

em-

employed their slaves to build churches, and allotted their lands to the endowment of those foundations. Kings gave to the church all that they had extorted from the people; and stripped themselves to such a degree, as even not to leave a sufficiency for the payment of the army, or for defraying the other charges of government. These deficiencies were never made up by those who were the cause of them. They bore no share in the maintenance of society. The payment of taxes with church money would have been a sacrilege, and a prostitution of holy things to profane purposes. Such was the declaration of the clergy, and the laity believed them. The possession of the third part of the feudal tenures in the kingdom, the free-will offerings of a deluded people, and the price set upon the priestly offices, did not satisfy the enormous avidity of the clergy, ever attentive to their own interest. They found in the Old Testament, that by divine appointment the priests had an undoubted right to the tithes of the produce of the land. This claim was so readily admitted, that they extended it to the tithe of industry, of the profits on trade, of the wages of labourers, of the pay of soldiers, and sometimes of the salaries of placemen.

 Rome, who at first was a silent spectator of these proceedings, and proudly enjoyed
the

the fuccefs that attended the rich and haughty apoftles of a Saviour born in obfcurity, and who died an ignominious death, foon coveted a fhare in the fpoils of England. The firft ftep fhe took was to open a trade for relics, which were always ufhered in with fome ftriking miracle, and fold in proportion to the credulity of the purchafers. The great men, and even monarchs, were invited to go in pilgrimage to the capital of the world, to purchafe a place in heaven fuitable to the rank they held on earth. The popes by degrees affumed the prefentation to church preferments, which at firft they gave away, but afterwards fold. By thefe means, their tribunal took cognizance of all ecclefiaftical caufes, and in time they claimed a tenth of the revenues of the clergy, who themfelves levied the tenth of all the fubftance of the realm.

When thefe pious extortions were carried as far as they poffibly could be in England, Rome afpired to the fupreme authority over it. The frauds of her ambition were covered with a facred veil. She fapped the foundations of liberty, but it was by employing the influence of opinion only. This was fetting up men in oppofition to themfelves, and availing herfelf of their prejudices in order to acquire an abfolute dominion over them. She ufurped the power of a defpotic judge between the altar and the throne, between

tween the prince and his subjects, between one potentate and another. She kindled the flames of war with her spiritual thunders. But she wanted emissaries to spread the terror of her arms, and made choice of the monks for that purpose. The secular clergy, notwithstanding their celibacy, which kept them from worldly connections, had still an attachment to the world by the ties of interest; often stronger than those of blood. A set of men, secluded from society by singular institutions which must incline them to fanaticism, and by a blind submission to the dictates of a foreign pontiff, were best adapted to second the views of such a sovereign. These vile and abject tools of superstition fulfilled their fatal employment but too successfully. With their intrigues, seconded by favourable occurrences, England, which had so long withstood the conquering arms of the ancient Roman empire, became tributary to modern Rome.

At length the passions and violent caprices of Henry VIII. broke the scandalous dependence. The abuse of so infamous a power had already opened the eyes of the nation. The prince ventured at once to shake off the authority of the pope, abolish monasteries, and assume the supremacy over his own church.

This open schism was followed by other alte-

alterations in the reign of Edward, son and successor to Henry. The religious opinions, which were then changing the face of Europe, were openly discussed. Something was taken from every one; many doctrines and rites of the old religion were retained; and from these several systems or tenets arose a new communion, distinguished by the name of The Church of England.

Elizabeth, who completed this important work, found theory alone too subtle; and thought it most expedient to captivate the senses, by the addition of some ceremonies. Her natural taste for grandeur, and the desire of putting a stop to the disputes about points of doctrine, by entertaining the eye with the external parade of worship, made her inclined to adopt a greater number of religious rites. But she was restrained by political considerations, and was obliged to sacrifice something to the prejudices of a party that had raised her to the throne, and was able to maintain her upon it.

Far from suspecting that James I. would execute what Elizabeth had not even dared to attempt, it might be expected that he would rather have been inclined to restrain ecclesiastical rites and ceremonies. That prince, who had been trained up in the principles of the Presbyterians, a sect who, with much spiritual pride, affected great simplicity

city of dress, gravity of manners, and austerity of doctrine, and loved to speak in scripture phrases, and to make use of none but scripture names for their children. One would have supposed that such an education must have prejudiced the king against the outward pomp of the catholic worship, and every thing that bore any affinity to it. But the spirit of system prevailed in him over the principles of education. Struck with the episcopal jurisdiction which he found established in England, and which he thought conformable to his own notions of civil government, he abandoned from conviction the early impressions he had received, and grew passionately fond of a hierarchy modelled upon the political œconomy of a well constituted empire. In this enthusiasm, he wanted to introduce this wonderful discipline into Scotland, his native country; and to unite to it a great many of the English, who still dissented from it. He even intended to add the pomp of the most awful ceremonies to the majestic plan, if he could have carried his grand projects into execution. But the opposition he met with at first setting out, woud not permit him to advance any further in his system of reformation. He contented himself with recommending to his son to resume his views, whenever the times should furnish a favourable opportunity; and represented

sented the Presbyterians to him as alike dangerous to religion and to the throne.

Charles readily adopted his advice, which was but too conformable to the principles of despotism he had imbibed from Buckingham his favourite, the most corrupt of men, and the corrupter of the courtiers. To pave the way to the revolution he was meditating, he promoted several bishops to the highest dignities in the government, and conferred on them most of the offices that gave the greatest influence on public measures. Those ambitious prelates, now become the masters of a prince who had been weak enough to be guided by the instigations of others, betrayed that ambition so familiar to the clergy, of raising up ecclesiastical jurisdiction under the shadow of the royal prerogative. They multiplied the church ceremonies without end, under pretence of their being of apostolical institution; and, to inforce their observance, had recourse to royal acts of arbitrary power.

It was evident that there was a settled design of restoring, in all its splendour, what the Protestants called Romish idolatry, though the most violent means should be necessary to compass it. This project gave the more umbrage, as it was supported by the prejudices and intrigues of a presumptuous queen, who had brought from France an

immo-

immoderate paffion for popery and arbitrary power.

It can scarce be imagined what acrimony these alarming sufpicions had raised in the minds of the people. Common prudence would have allowed time for the ferment to subside. But the spirit of fanaticism made choice of those troublesome times to recall every thing to the unity of the church of England, which was become more odious to the diffenters, since so many customs had been introduced into it which they confidered as superstitious. An order was issued, that both kingdoms should conform to the worship and discipline of the episcopal church. This law included, the Presbyterians, who then began to be called Puritans, because they profeffed to take the pure and simple word of God for the rule of their faith and practice. It was extended likewife to all the foreign Calvinifts that were in the kingdom, whatever difference there might be in their opinions. This hierarchal worship was enjoined to the regiments, and trading companies, that were in the feveral countries in Europe. Laftly, the English ambaffadors were required to feparate from all communion with the foreign proteftants; so that England loft all the influence she had abroad, as the head and fupport of the reformation.

In

In this fatal crisis, most of the Puritans were divided between submission and opposition. Those who would neither stoop to yield, nor take the pains to resist, turned their views towards North-America, to seek for that civil and religious liberty which their ungrateful country denied them. The enemies of their peace attempted to shut this retreat against these devout fugitives, who wanted to worship God in their own way in a desert land. Eight ships that lay at anchor in the Thames ready to sail, were stopped; and Cromwell is said to have been detained there by that very king whom he afterwards brought to the scaffold. Enthusiasm, however, stronger than the rage of persecution, surmounted every obstacle; and that region of America was soon filled with presbyterians. The comfort they enjoyed in their retreat, gradually induced all those of their party to follow them, who were not attrocious enough to take delight in those dreadful catastrophes which soon after made England a scene of blood and horror. Many were afterwards induced to remove thither in more peaceable times, with a view to advance their fortunes. In a word, all Europe contributed greatly to increase their population. Thousands of unhappy men, oppressed by the tyranny or intolerant spirit of their sovereign, took refuge in that hemisphere.

Let us now endeavour to acquire some information respecting that country.

3. *Parallel between the Old and the New World.*

It is surprising that for so long a time so little should have been known of the new world even after it was discovered. Barbarous soldiers and rapacious merchants were not proper persons to give us just and clear notions of this half of the universe. It was the province of philosophy alone to avail itself of the informations scattered in the accounts of voyagers and missionaries, in order to see America such as nature hath made it, and to investigate its affinity with the rest of the globe.

It is now pretty certain, that the new continent has not half the extent of surface as the old. On the other hand, the form of both is so singularly alike, that we might easily be seduced to draw consequences from this particular, if it were always not right to be upon our guard against the spirit of system, which often stops us in our researches after truth, and hinders us from attaining to it.

The two continents seem to form as it were two broad slips of land that begin from the arctic pole, and terminate at the tropic of Capricorn, parted on the east and west by the ocean that surrounds them. Whatever may be the structure of these two continents, and the balance or symmetry of their form, it is plain their equilibrium does not depend upon their position. It is the inconstancy of the sea that makes the solidity of the earth. To fix the globe upon its basis, it seemed necessary to have an element which, floating incessantly round our planet, might by its weight counterbalance all other substances, and by its fluidity restore that equilibrium which the conflict of the other elements might have overthrown. Water, by the motion that is natural to it, and by its gravity likewise, is infinitely better calculated to keep up that harmony and that balance of the several parts round its centre. If our hemisphere has a very wide extent of land to the north, a mass of water of equal weight at the opposite part will certainly produce an equilibrium. If under the tropics we have a rich country covered with men and animals; under the same latitude, America will have a sea full of fish. Whilst forests of trees bending under the largest fruits, the most enormous quadrupeds, the most populous nations, elephants and men, press on the surface of the earth, and seem to absorb all its fertility throughout the torrid zone; at both poles, are found the whales, with innumerable multitudes of cods and herrings, with clouds of insects, and all the infinite

and

and prodigious tribes that inhabit the seas, as if to support the axis of the earth, and prevent its inclining or deviating to either side; if, however, elephants, whales, or men, can be said to have any weight on a globe, where all living creatures are but a transient modification of the earth that composes it. In a word, the ocean rolls over this globe to fashion it, in conformity to the general laws of gravity. Sometimes it covers and sometimes it uncovers a hemisphere, a pole, or a zone; but in general it seems to affect more particularly the equator, as the cold of the poles in some measure takes off that fluidity which constitutes its essence, and imparts to it all its action. It is chiefly between the tropics that the sea spreads and is in motion, and that it undergoes the greatest change both in its regular and periodical motions, as well as in those kinds of convulsions occasionally excited in it by tempestuous winds. The attraction of the sun, and the fermentations occasioned by its continual heat in the torrid zone, must have a very remarkable influence upon the ocean. The motion of the moon adds a new force to this influence; and the sea, to yield to this double impulse, must, it should seem, flow towards the equator. The flatness of the globe towards the poles can only be ascribed to that great extent of water that has hitherto prevented our knowing

any

any thing of the lands near the south pole. The sea cannot easily pass from within the tropics, if the temperate and frozen zones are not nearer the centre of the earth than the torrid zone. It is the sea then that constitutes the equilibrium with the land, and disposes the arrangement of the materials that compose it. One proof that the two regular slips of land which the two continents of the globe present at first view are not essentially necessary to its conformation, is, that the new hemisphere has remained covered with the waters of the sea a much longer time than the old. Besides, if there is a visible affinity between the two hemispheres, there may be differences between them as striking as the similitude is, which will destroy that supposed harmony we flatter ourselves that we shall find.

When we consider the map of the world, and see the local correspondence there is between the isthmus of Suez and that of Panama, between the cape of Good Hope and cape Horn, between the Archipelago of the East-Indies and that of the Leeward Islands, and between the mountains of Chili and those of Monomotapa, we are struck with the similarity of the several forms this picture presents. Every where we imagine we see land opposite to land, water to water, islands and peninsulas scattered by the hand of nature

to

to serve as a counterpoise, and the sea by its fluctuation constantly maintaining the balance of the whole. But if, on the other hand, we compare the great extent of the Pacific Ocean, which parts the East and West Indies, with the small space the Ocean occupies between the coast of Guinea and that of Brasil; the vast quantity of inhabited land to the North, with the little we know towards the South; the direction of the mountains of Tartary and Europe, which is from East to West, with that of the Cordileras which run from North to South; the mind is at a stand, and we have the mortification to see the order and symmetry vanish with which we had embellished our system of the earth. The observer is still more displeased with his conjectures, when he considers the immense height of the mountains of Peru. Then, indeed, he is astonished to see a continent so high and so lately discovered, the sea so far below its tops, and so recently come down from the lands that seemed to be effectually defended from its attacks by those tremendous bulwarks. It is, however, an undeniable fact, that both continents of the new hemisphere have been covered with the sea. The air and the land confirm this truth.

The broad and long rivers of America; the immense forests to the South; the spacious lakes

lakes and vast morasses to the North; the eternal snows between the tropics; few of those pure sands that seem to be the remains of an exhausted ground; no men entirely black; very fair people under the line; a cool and mild air in the same latitude as the sultry and uninhabitable parts of Africa; a frozen and severe climate under the same parallel as our temperate climates; and, lastly, a difference of ten or twelve degrees in the temperature of the old and new hemispheres; these are so many tokens of a world that is still in its infancy.

 Why should the continent of America be so much warmer and so much colder in proportion than that of Europe, if it were not for the moisture the ocean has left behind, by quitting it long after our continent was peopled? Nothing but the sea can possibly have prevented Mexico from being inhabited as early as Asia. If the waters that still moisten the bowels of the earth in the new hemisphere had not covered its surface, man would very early have cut down the woods, drained the fens, consolidated a soft and watery soil by stirring it up and exposing it to the rays of the sun, opened a free passage to the winds, and raised dikes along the rivers: in short, the climate would have been totally altered by this time. But a rude and unpeopled hemisphere denotes a recent world;

world; when the sea, rolling in the neighbourhood of its coasts, still flows obscurely in its channels. The sun less scorching, more plentiful rains, and thicker and more stagnating vapours, betray either the decay or the infancy of nature.

The difference of climate, arising from the waters having lain so long on the ground in America, could not but have a great influence on men and animals. From this diversity of causes must necessarily arise a very great diversity of effects. Accordingly we see more species of animals, by two thirds, in the old continent than in the new; animals of the same kind considerably larger; fiercer and more savage monsters, in proportion to the greater increase of mankind. On the other hand, nature seems to have strangely neglected the new world. The men have less strength and less courage; no beard and no hair: they are degraded in all the tokens of manhood; and but little susceptible of the lively and powerful sentiment of love, which is the principle of every attachment, the first instinct, the first band of society, without which all the other factitious ties have neither energy nor duration. The women, who are still more weak, are neither favourably treated by nature nor by the men, who have but little love for them, and consider them as the instruments that are to furnish to their wants;

they rather facrifice them to their own indolence, than confecrate them to their pleafures. This indolence is the great delight and fupreme felicity of the Americans, of which the women are the victims by the continual labours impofed upon them. It muft, however, be confeffed, that in America, as in all other parts, the men, when they have fentenced the women to work, have been fo equitable as to take upon themfelves the perils of war, together with the toils of hunting and fifhing. But their indifference for the fex which nature has intrufted with the care of reproducing the fpecies, implies an imperfection in their organs, a fort of ftate of childhood in the people of America, as in thofe of our continent who are not yet arrived to the age of puberty. This is a radical vice in the other hemifphere, the recency of which is difcovered by this kind of imperfection.

But if the Americans are new people, are they a race of men originally diftinct from thofe that cover the face of the old world? This is a queftion which ought not to be haftily decided. The origin of the population of America is involved in inextricable difficulties. If we affert that the Greenlanders firft came from Norway, and then went over to the coaft of Labrador; others will tell us, it is more natural to fuppofe that the Greenlanders

landers are sprung from the Esquimaux, to whom they bear a greater resemblance than to the Europeans. If we should suppose that California was peopled from Kamtschatka, it may be asked what motive or what chance could have led the Tartars to the north-west of America. Yet it is imagined to be from Greenland or from Kamtschatka that the inhabitants of the old world must have gone over to the new, as it is by those two countries that the two continents are connected, or at least approach nearest to one another. Besides, how can we conceive that in America the torrid zone can have been peopled from one of the frozen zones? Population will indeed spread from north to south; but it must naturally have begun under the equator, where life is cherished by warmth. If the people of America could not come from our continent, and yet appear to be a new race, we must have recourse to the flood, which is the source and the solution of all difficulties in the history of nations.

Let us suppose, that the sea having overflowed the other hemisphere, its old inhabitants took refuge upon the Apalachian mountains, and the Cordileras, which are far higher than our mount Ararat. But how could they have lived upon those heights, covered with snow, and surrounded with waters? How is it possible, that men, who
had

had breathed in a pure and delightful climate, could have survived the miseries of want, the inclemency of a tainted air, and those numberless calamities which must be the unavoidable consequences of a deluge? How will the race have been preserved and propagated in those times of general calamity, and in the succeeding ages of a languid existence? In defiance of all these obstacles, we must allow that America has been peopled by these wretched remains of the great devastation. Every thing carries the vestiges of a malady, of which the human race still feels the effects. The ruin of that world is still imprinted on its inhabitants. They are a species of men degraded and degenerated in their natural constitution, in their stature, in their way of life, and in their understandings, which have made so little progress in all the arts of civilization. A damper air, and a more marshy ground, must necessarily infect the very roots and feeds both of the subsistence and multiplication of mankind. It must have required some ages to restore population, and still a greater number before the ground could be settled and dried so as to be fit for tillage and for the foundation of buildings. The earth must necessarily be purified before the air could clear, and the air must be clear before the earth could be rendered habitable.
The

The imperfection therefore of nature in America is not a proof of its recent origin, but of its regeneration. It was probably peopled at the same time as the other hemisphere, but may have been overflown later. The large fossil bones that are found under ground in America, shew that it formerly had elephants, rhinoceroses, and other enormous quadrupeds, which have since disappeared from those regions. The gold and silver mines that are found just below the surface, are signs of a very ancient revolution of the globe, but later than those that have overturned our hemisphere.

Suppose America had, by some means or other, been repeopled by our roving hords, that period would be so remote, that it would still give great antiquity to the inhabitants of that hemisphere. Three or four centuries will not then be sufficient to allow for the foundation of the empires of Mexico and Peru; for though we find no trace in these countries of our arts, or of the opinions and customs that prevail in other parts of the globe, yet we have found a police and a society established, inventions and practices, which, though they did not shew any marks of times anterior to the deluge, yet they implied a long series of ages subsequent to this catastrophe. For though in Mexico, as in Egypt, a country surrounded with waters,

moun-

mountains, and other invincible obstacles, must have forced the men inclosed in it to unite after a time, though they might at first live in altercations and in continual and bloody wars, yet it was only in process of time that they could invent and establish a worship and a legislation, which they could not possibly have borrowed from remote times or countries. The single art of speech, and that of writing, though but in hieroglyphics, required more ages to train up an unconnected nation that must have created both those arts, than it would take up days to perfect a child in both. Ages bear not the same proportion to the whole race as years do to individuals. The former is to occupy a vast field, both as to space and duration; while the other has only some moments or instants of time to fill up, or rather to run over. The likeness and uniformity observable in the features and manners of the American nations, plainly shew that they are not so ancient as those of our continent which differ so much from each other; but at the same time this circumstance seems to confirm that they did not proceed from any foreign hemisphere, with which they have no kind of affinity that can indicate an immediate descent.

4. *Com-*

4. *Comparison between civilized people and savages.*

WHATEVER may be the case with regard to their origin or their antiquity, which are both uncertain, a more interesting object of inquiry, perhaps, is, to determine whether these untutored nations are more or less happy than our civilized people. Let us, therefore, examine whether the condition of rude man left to mere animal instinct, whose day, which is spent in hunting, feeding, producing his species, and reposing himself, is the model of all the rest of his days, is better or worse than the condition of that wonderful being, who makes his bed of down, spins and weaves the thread of the silk-worm to clothe himself, has exchanged the cave, his original abode, for a palace, and has varied his indulgences and his wants in a thousand different ways.

It is in the nature of man that we must look for his means of happiness. What does he want to be as happy as he can be? Present subsistence; and, if he thinks of futurity, the hopes and certainty of enjoying that blessing. The savage, who has not been driven to the frigid zones, is not in want of this first of necessaries. If he lays in no stores, it is because the earth and the sea are reservoirs al-

ways

ways open to supply his wants. Fish and game are to be had all the year, and will make up for the deficiency of the dead seasons. The savage has no close houses, or commodious fire-places; but his furs answer all the purposes of the roof, the garment, and the stove. He works but for his own benefit, sleeps when he is weary, and is a stranger to watchings and restless nights. War is a matter of choice to him. Danger, like labour, is a condition of his nature, not a profession annexed to his birth; a duty of the nation, not a family bondage. The savage is serious, but not melancholy; and his countenance seldom bears the impression of those passions and disorders that leave such shocking and fatal marks on ours. He cannot feel the want of what he does not desire, nor can he desire what he is ignorant of. Most of the conveniencies of life are remedies for evils he does not feel. Pleasures are a relief to appetites which are not excited in his sensations. He seldom experiences any of that weariness that arises from unsatisfied desires, or that emptiness and uneasiness of mind that is the offspring of prejudice and vanity. In a word, the savage is subject to none but natural evils.

But what greater happiness than this does the civilized man enjoy? His food is more wholesome and delicate than that of the savage.

vage. He has softer clothes, and a habitation better secured against the inclemencies of the weather. But the common people, who are to be the basis and object of civil society, those numbers of men who in all states bear the burden of hard labour, cannot be said to live happy, either in those empires where the consequences of war and the imperfection of the police has reduced them to a state of slavery, or in those governments where the progress of luxury and policy has reduced them to a state of servitude. The mixed governments sometimes afford some sparks of happiness, founded on a shadow of liberty; but this happiness is purchased by torrents of blood, which repel tyranny for a time only to let it fall the heavier upon the devoted nation, sooner or later doomed to oppression. Let us but observe how Caligula and Nero have revenged the expulsion of the Tarquins and the death of Cæsar.

Tyranny, we are told, is the work of the people, and not of kings. But if so, why do they suffer it? Why do they not repel the encroachments of despotism; and while it employs violence and artifice to enslave all the faculties of men, why do they not oppose it with all their powers? But is it lawful to murmur and complain under the rod of the oppressor? Will it not exasperate and provoke him to pursue the victim to death?

The

The cries of servitude he calls rebellion; and they are to be stifled in a dungeon, and sometimes on a scaffold. The man who should assert the rights of man, would perish in neglect and infamy. Tyranny, therefore, must be endured, under the name of authority.

If so, to what outrages is not the civilized man exposed! If he is possessed of any property, he knows not how far he may call it his own, when he must divide the produce between the courtier who may attack his estate, the lawyer who must be paid for teaching him how to preserve it, the soldier who may lay it waste, and the collector who comes to levy unlimited taxes. If he has no property, how can he be assured of a permanent subsistence? What species of industry is there secured against the vicissitudes of fortune, and the encroachments of government?

In the forests of America, if there is a scarcity in the north, the savages bend their course to the south. The wind or the sun will drive a wandering clan to more temperate climates. Between the gates and bars that shut up our civilized states, if famine, war, or pestilence, should consume an empire, it is a prison where all must expect to perish in misery, or in the horrors of slaughter. The man who is unfortunately born there must endure all extortions, all the severities,

verities, that the inclemency of the seasons and the injustice of government may bring upon him.]

In our provinces, the vassal, or free mercenary, digs and ploughs the whole year round, on lands that are not his own, and whose produce does not belong to him; and he is even happy, if his assiduous labour procures him a share of the crops he has sown and reaped. Observed and harrassed by a hard and restless landlord, who grudges him the very straw on which he rests his weary limbs, the wretch is daily exposed to diseases, which, joined to his poverty, make him wish for death, rather than for an expensive cure, followed by infirmities and toil. Whether tenant or subject, he is doubly a slave: if he has a few acres, his lord comes and gathers where he has not sown; if he is worth but a yoke of oxen or a pair of horses, he must go with them upon services; if he has nothing but his person, the prince takes him for a soldier. Every where he meets with masters, and always with oppression.

In our cities, the workman and the artist who have establishments are at the mercy of greedy and idle masters, who by the privilege of monopoly have purchased of government a power of making industry work for nothing, and of selling its labours at a very high price. The lower class have no more than the sight of that luxury of which they are doubly the victims, by the watchings and fatigues it occasions them, and by the insolence of the pomp that mortifies and tramples upon them.

Even supposing that the dangerous labours of our quarries, mines, and forges, with all the arts that are performed by fire, and that perils of navigation and commerce were less pernicious than the roving life of the savages, who live upon hunting and fishing; suppose that men, who are ever lamenting the sorrows and affronts that arise merely from opinion, are less unhappy than the savages, who never shed a tear in the midst of the most excruciating tortures; there would still remain a wide difference between the fate of the civilized man and the wild Indian, a difference entirely to the disadvantage of social life. This is the injustice that reigns in the partial distribution of fortunes and stations; an inequality which is at once the effect and the cause of oppression.

In vain does custom, prejudice, ignorance, and hard labour, stupify the lower class of mankind, so as to render them insensible of their degradation; neither religion nor morality can hinder them from seeing and feeling the injustice of political order in the distribution of good and evil. How often have we heard the poor man expostulating with Heaven, and asking what he had done, that he he should deserve to be born in an indigent and dependent station. Even if great conflicts were inseparable from more exalted stations, which might be sufficient to balance all the advantages and all the superiority that the social state claims over the state of nature, still the obscure man, who is unacquainted with those conflicts, sees nothing in a high rank but that affluence which is the cause of his own poverty. He envies the rich man those pleasures to which he is so accustomed, that he has lost all relish for them. What domestic can have a real affection for his master, or what is the attachment of a servant? Was ever any prince truly beloved by his courtiers, even when he was hated by his subjects? If we prefer our condition to that of the savages, it is because civil life has made us incapable of bearing some natural hardships which the savage is more exposed to than we are, and because we are attached to some indulgences that custom has made necessary to us. Even in the vigour of life, a civilized man may accustom himself to live among savages, and return to the state of nature. We have an instance of this in that Scotchman who was cast away on the island of Fernandez, where he lived alone, and was happy as soon as he was so taken up with supplying his wants, as to forget his own country, his language, his name,

name, and even the utterance of words. After four years, he felt himself eased of the burden of social life, when he had lost all reflection or thought of the past, and all anxiety for the future.

Lastly, the consciousness of independence being one of the first instincts in man, he who enjoys this primitive right, with a moral certainty of a competent subsistence, is incomparably happier than the rich man, restrained by laws, masters, prejudices, and fashions, which incessantly remind him of the loss of his liberty. To compare the state of the savages to that of children, is to decide at once the question that has been so warmly debated by philosophers, concerning the advantages of the state of nature, and that of social life. Children, notwithstanding the restraints of education, are in the happiest age of human life. Their habitual cheerfulness, when they are not under the schoolmaster's rod, is the surest indication of the happiness they feel. After all, a single word may determine this great question. Let us ask the civilized man, whether he is happy; and the savage, whether he is unhappy. If they both answer in the negative, the dispute is at an end.

Civilized nations, this parallel must certainly be mortifying to you: but you cannot too strongly feel the weight of the calamities

under

under which you groan. The more painful this senfation is, the more will it awaken your attention to the true caufes of your fufferings. You may at laft be convinced that they proceed from the confufion of your opinions, from the defects of your political conftitutions, and from capricious laws, which are in continual oppofition to the laws of nature.

After this inquiry into the moral ftate of the Americans, let us return to the natural ftate of their country. Let us fee what it was before the arrival of the Englifh, and what it is become under their dominion.

5. *In what ftate the Englifh found North America, and what they have done there.*

THE firft Europeans who went over to fettle Englifh colonies, found immenfe forefts. The vaft trees, that grew up to the clouds, were fo encumbered with creeping plants, that they could not be got at. The wild beafts made thefe woods ftill more inacceffible. They met only with a few favages, clothed with the fkins of thofe monfters. The human race, thinly fcattered, fled from each other, or purfued only with intent to deftroy. The earth feemed ufelefs to man; and its powers were not exerted fo much for his fupport, as in the breeding of animals,

more

more obedient to the laws of nature. The earth produced every thing at pleasure, without assistance, and without direction; it yielded all its bounties with uncontrolled profusion for the benefit of all, not for the pleasure or conveniences of one species of beings. The rivers now glided freely thro' the forests; now spread themselves quietly in a wide morass; from hence issuing in various streams, they formed a multitude of islands, encompassed with their channels. The spring was restored from the spoils of autumn. The leaves dried and rotted at the foot of the trees, supplied them with fresh sap to enable them to shoot out new blossoms. The hollow trunks of trees afforded a retreat to prodigious flights of birds. The sea, dashing against the coasts, and indenting the gulphs, threw up shoals of amphibious monsters, enormous whales, crabs and turtles, that sported uncontrolled on the desert shores. There nature exerted her plastic power, incessantly producing the gigantic inhabitants of the ocean, and asserting the freedom of the earth and the sea.

But man appeared, and immediately changed the face of North America. He introduced symmetry, by the assistance of all the instruments of art. The impenetrable woods were instantly cleared, and made room for commodious habitations. The wild beasts
were

were driven away, and flocks of domeftic animals fupplied their place; whilft thorns and briars made way for rich harvefts. The waters forfook part of their domain, and were drained off into the interior parts of the land, or into the fea, by deep canals. The coafts were covered with towns, and the bays with fhips; and thus the new world, like the old, became fubject to man. What powerful engines have raifed that wonderful ftructure of European induftry and policy? Let us proceed to the particulars.

BOOK I.

ENGLISH COLONIES SETTLED AT HUDSON's BAY, NEWFOUNDLAND, NOVA SCOTIA, NEW ENGLAND, NEW YORK, AND NEW JERSEY.

CHAP. I.
Of Hudson's Bay.

1. *Climate. Customs of the inhabitants. Trade.*

IN the remotest part stands a solitary object, distinct from the whole, which is called Hudson's bay. This bay, of about ten degrees in length, is formed by the ocean in the distant and northern parts of America. The breadth of the entrance is about six leagues; but it is only to be attempted from the beginning of July to the end of September, and is even then extremely dangerous. This danger arises from mountains of ice, some of which are said to be from 15 to 18 hundred feet thick, and which having been produced by winters of five or six years duration in little gulphs

gulphs constantly filled with snow, are forced out of them by north-west winds, or by some other extraordinary cause. The best way of avoiding them is to keep as near as possible to the northern coast, which must necessarily be less obstructed and most free by the natural directions of both winds and currents.

 The north-west wind, which blows almost constantly in winter, and very often in summer, frequently raises violent storms within the bay itself, which is rendered still more dangerous by the number of shoals that are found there. Happily, however, small groups of islands are met with at different distances, which are of a sufficient height to afford a shelter from the storm. Besides these small Archipelagos, there are in many places large piles of bare rock; but, except the Alga Marina, the bay produces as few vegetables as the other northern seas. Throughout all the countries surrounding this bay, the sun never rises or sets without forming a great cone of light; this phenomenon is succeeded by the Aurora Borealis, which tinges the hemisphere with coloured rays of such a brilliancy, that the splendour of them is not effaced even by that of the full moon. Notwithstanding this, there is seldom a bright sky. In spring and autumn, the air is always filled with thick fogs; and in winter, with an infinite number of small icicles.

Though

Though the heats in the summer are pretty considerable for six weeks or two months, there is seldom any thunder or lightning, owing, no doubt, to the great number of sulphureous exhalations, which, however, are sometimes set on fire by the Aurora Borealis; and this light flame consumes the barks of the trees, but leaves their trunks untouched.

One of the effects of the extreme cold or snow that prevails in this climate, is that of turning those animals white in winter, which are naturally brown or grey. Nature has bestowed upon them all, soft, long, and thick furs, the hair of which falls off as the weather grows milder. In most of these quadrupeds, the feet, the tail, the ears, and generally speaking all those parts in which the circulation is slower because they are most remote from the heart, are extremely short. Wherever they happen to be somewhat longer, they are proportionably well covered. Under this heavy sky, all liquors become solid by freezing, and break whatever vessels contain them. Even spirits of wine loses its fluidity. It is not uncommon to see fragments of large rocks loosened and detached from the great mass, by the force of the frost. All these phenomena, common enough during the whole winter, are much more terrible at the new and full moon, which in these regions has an influence upon the weather,

ther, the caufes of which are not known.

In this frozen zone, iron, lead, copper, marble, and a fubftance refembling fea-coal, have been difcovered. In other refpects, the foil is extremely barren. Except the coafts, which are for the moft part marfhy, where there grows a little grafs and fome foft wood, the reft of the country offers nothing but very high mofs and a few weak fhrubs thinly fcattered.

This fterility of nature extends itfelf to every thing. The human race are few in number, and fcarce any of its individuals above four feet high. Their heads bear the fame enormous proportion to the reft of their bodies, as thofe of children do. The fmallnefs of their feet makes them aukward and tottering in their gait. Small hands and a round mouth, which in Europe are reckoned a beauty, feem almoft a deformity in thefe people, becaufe we fee nothing here but the effects of a weak organization, and of a cold that contracts and reftrains the fprings of growth, and is fatal to the progrefs of animal as well as of vegetable life. Befides this, all their men, though they have neither hair nor beard, have the appearance of being old. This is partly occafioned from the formation of their lower lip, which is thick, flefhy, and projecting beyond the upper. Such are the Efquimaux, which inhabit not only the coaft of Labrador, from whence they have taken
their

their name, but likewise all that tract of country which extends itself from the point of Belle-Isle to the most northern parts of America.

The inhabitants of Hudson's bay have, like the Greenlanders, a flat face, with short but flattened noses, the pupil of their eyes yellow and the iris black. Their women have marks of deformity peculiar to their sex; amongst others, very long and flabby breasts. This defect, which is not natural, arises from their custom of giving suck to their children till they are five or six years old. The children pull their mothers breasts with their hands, and almost suspend themselves by them.

It is not true that there are races of the Esquimaux entirely black, as has been since supposed, and afterwards accounted for; nor that they live under ground. How should they dig into a soil, which the cold renders harder than stone? How is it possible they should live in caverns where they would be infallibly drowned by the first melting of the snows? What, however, is certain, and almost equally surprising, is, that they spend the winter under huts run up in haste, and made of flints joined together with cements of ice, where they live without any other fire but that of a lamp hung up in the middle of the shed, for the purpose of dressing their game and the fish they feed upon. The heat

of

of their blood, and of their breath, added to the vapour arising from this small flame, is sufficient to make their huts as hot as stoves.

The Esquimaux dwell constantly near the sea, which supplies them with all their provisions. Both their constitution and complexion partake of the quality of their food. The flesh of the seal is their food, and the oil of the whale is their drink; which produces in them all an olive complexion, a strong smell of fish, an oily and tenacious sweat, and sometimes a sort of scaly leprosy. This last is, probably, the reason why the mothers have the same custom as the bears, of licking their young ones.

This nation, weak and degraded by nature, is notwithstanding most intrepid upon a sea that is constantly dangerous. In boats made and sewed together in the same manner as goat-skin bottles, but at the same time so well closed that it is impossible for water to penetrate them, they follow the shoals of herrings thro' the whole of their polar emigrations, and attack the whales and seals at the peril of their lives. One stroke of the whale's tail is sufficient to drown a hundred of them, and the seal is armed with teeth to devour those he cannot drown; but the hunger of the Esquimaux is superior to the rage of these monsters. They have an inordinate thirst for the whale's oil; which is necessary to preserve the heat in

their

their stomachs, and defend them from the severity of the cold. Indeed whales, men, birds, and all the quadrupeds and fish of the north, are supplied by nature with a degree of fat which prevents the muscles from freezing, and the blood from coagulating. Every thing in these arctic regions is either oily or gummy, and even the trees are resinous.

The Esquimaux are notwithstanding subject to two fatal disorders; the scurvy, and the loss of sight. The continuation of the snows on the ground, joined to the reverberation of the rays of the sun on the ice, dazzle their eyes in such a manner, that they are almost constantly obliged to wear shades made of very thin wood, through which small apertures for the light have been bored with fishbones. Doomed to a six-months night, they never see the sun but obliquely; and then it seems rather to blind them, than to give them light. Sight, the most delightful blessing of nature, is a fatal gift to them, and they are generally deprived of it when young.

A still more cruel evil, which is the scurvy, consumes them by slow degrees. It insinuates itself into their blood, changes, thickens, and impoverishes the whole mass. The fogs of the sea, which they inspire; the dense and inelastic air they breathe in their huts, which are shut up from all communication with the external air; the continued and tedious inactivity

tivity of their winters; a mode of life alternately roving and sedentary; every thing, in short, serves to increase this dreadful illness; which in a little time becomes contagious, and, spreading itself throughout their habitations, is but too probably transmitted by the means of generation.

Notwithstanding these inconveniences, the Esquimaux is so passionately fond of his country, that no inhabitant of the most favoured spot under heaven quits it with more reluctance than he does his frozen deserts. One of the reasons of it may be, that he finds it difficult to breathe in a softer and cooler climate. The sky of Amsterdam, Copenhagen, and London, though constantly obscured by thick and fetid vapours, is too clear for an Esquimaux. Perhaps, too, there may be something in the change of life and manners still more contrary to the health of savages than the climate. It is not impossible but that the indulgences of an European may be a poison to the Esquimaux.

Such were the inhabitants of the country discovered in 1610 by Henry Hudson. This intrepid mariner, in searching after a north-west passage to the south-seas, discovered three streights, through which he hoped to find out a new way to Asia by America. He sailed boldly into the midst of the new gulph; and was preparing to explore all its parts,
when

when his treacherous ship's company put him into the long-boat, with seven others, and left him without either arms or provisions exposed to all the dangers both of sea and land. The barbarians, who refused him the necessaries of life, could not, however, rob him of the honour of the discovery; and the bay which he first found out will ever be called by his name.

The miseries of the civil war which followed soon after, had, however, made the English forget this distant country, which had nothing to attract them. More quiet times had not yet brought it to their remembrance, when Groseillers and Radisson, two French Canadians, who had met with some discontent at home, informed the English, who were engaged in repairing by trade the mischiefs of discord, of the profits arising from furs, and of their claim to the country that furnished them. Those who proposed the business shewed so much ability, that they were intrusted with the execution; and the first establishment they formed succeeded so well, that it surpassed their own hopes as well as their promises.

This success alarmed the French; who were afraid, and with reason, that most of the fine furs which they got from the northern parts of Canada, would be carried to Hudson's bay. Their alarms were confirmed
by

by the unanimous teftimony of their Coureurs de Bois, who fince 1656 had been four times as far as the borders of the ftrait. It would have been a defirable thing to have gone by the fame road to attack the new colony; but the diftance being thought too confiderable, notwithftanding the convenience of the rivers, it was at length determined that the expedition fhould be made by fea. The fate of it was trufted to Grofeillers and Radiffon, who had been eafily brought back to a regard for their country.

Thefe two bold and reftlefs men failed from Quebec in 1682, upon two veffels badly fitted out; but on their arrival, finding themfelves not ftrong enough to attack the enemy, they were contented with erecting a fort in the neighbourhood of that they thought to have taken. From this time there began a rivalfhip between the two companies, one fettled at Canada, the other in England, for the exclufive trade of the bay, which was conftantly fed by the difputes it gave birth to, till at laft, after each of their fettlements had been frequently taken by the other, all hoftilities were terminated by the treaty of Utrecht, which gave up the whole to Great Britain.

Hudfon's Bay, properly fpeaking, is only a mart for trade. The feverity of the climate

mate having destroyed all the corn sown there at different times, has frustrated every hope of agriculture, and consequently of population. Throughout the whole of this extensive coast, there are not more than ninety or a hundred soldiers, or factors, comprised in four bad forts, of which York fort is the principal. Their business is to receive the furs which the neighbouring savages bring in exchange for merchandise, of which they have been taught the value and use.

Though these skins are of much more value than those which come out of countries not so far north, yet they are cheaper. The savages give ten beaver skins for a gun, two for a pound of powder, one for four pounds of lead, one for a hatchet, one for six knives, two for a pound of glass beads, six for a cloth coat, five for a petticoat, and one for a pound of snuff. Combs, looking-glasses, kettles, and brandy, sell in proportion. As the beaver is the common measure of exchange, by another regulation as fraudulent as the first, two otter's skins and three martins are required instead of one beaver. Besides this tyranny, which is authorised, there is another which is at least tolerated, by which the savages are constantly defrauded in the quality, quantity, and measure of what is given them; and the fraud amounts to about one third of the value.

From

From this regular fyftem of impofition it is eafy to guefs that the commerce of Hudfon's bay is a monopoly. The capital of the company that is in poffeffion of it was originally no more than 10,565 l. 12 s. 6 d. and has been fucceffively increafed to 104,146 l. 12 s. 6 d. This capital brings them in an annual return of forty or fifty thoufand fkins of beavers or other animals, upon which they make fo exorbitant a profit, that it excites the jealoufy and clamours of the nation. Two thirds of thefe beautiful furs are either confumed in kind in the three kingdoms, or made ufe of in the national manufactures. The reft are carried into Germany, where the climate makes them a valuable commodity.

2. *Whether there is a paffage at Hudfon's Bay leading to the Eaft Indies.*

But it is neither the acquifition of thefe favage riches, nor the ftill greater emoluments that might be drawn from this trade if it were made free, which has fixed the attention of England as well as that of all Europe upon this frozen continent. Hudfon's bay always has been and is ftill looked upon as the neareft road from Europe to the Eaft-Indies, and to the richeft parts of Afia.

Cabot was the firft who entertained an idea of a north-weft paffage to the fouth feas;

seas; but his discoveries ended at Newfoundland. After him followed a crowd of English navigators, many of whom had the glory of giving their names to savage coasts which no mortal had ever visited before. These bold and memorable expeditions were more brilliant than really useful. The most fortunate of them did not ever furnish a fresh conjecture on the end that was proposed. The Dutch, less frequent in their trials, less animated in the means by which they pursued them, were of course not more successful, and the whole began to be treated as a chimæra, when the discovery of Hudson's Bay rekindled all the hopes that were nearly extinguished.

At this period the attempts were renewed with fresh ardour. Those that had been made before in vain by the mother country, now taken up with her own intestine commotions, were pursued by New England, whose situation was favourable to the enterprize. Still, however, for some time there were more voyages undertaken than discoveries made. The nation was a long time kept in suspense by the different accounts of the adventures divided amongst themselves. While some maintained the possibility, others the probability, and others again asserted the certainty, of the passage; the accounts they gave, instead of clearing up the point, involved

ved it in still greater darkness. Indeed, these accounts are so full of obscurity and confusion, so many things are concealed in them, and they display such visible marks of ignorance and want of veracity, that with the utmost desire of deciding, it is impossible to build any thing like a solid judgment upon testimonies so suspicious. At length, the famous expedition of 1746 threw some kind of light upon a point which had remained inveloped in darkness for two centuries past. But upon what grounds have the later navigators taken up better hopes? What are the experiments on which they found their conjectures? Let us proceed to give an account of their arguments. There are three facts in natural history, which henceforward must be taken for granted. The first is, that the tides come from the ocean, and that they extend more or less into the other seas, in proportion as their channels communicate with the great reservoirs by larger or smaller openings; whence it follows, that this periodical motion is scarce perceptible in the Mediterranean, in the Baltic, and in other gulphs of the same nature. A second matter of fact is, that the tides are much later and much weaker in places more remote from the ocean, than in those which are nearer to it. The third fact is, that violent winds, which blow in a direction with the tides, make them rise above their ordinary boundaries; and that those which blow in a contrary direction retard the motion of the tides, at the same time that they diminish their swell.

From these principles, it is most certain, that if Hudson's bay were no more than a gulph inclosed between two continents, and had no communication but with the Atlantic, the tides in it would be very inconsiderable; they would be weaker in proportion as they were further removed from the source, and they would be much less strong whereever they had to resist opposite winds. But it is proved by observations made with the greatest skill and precision, that the tides are very high throughout the whole of the bay. It is certain that they are higher towards the bottom than even at the very mouth of the bay, or at least in the neighbourhood of it. It is proved, that even this height increases whenever the wind blows from a corner opposite to the streight. It is, therefore, certain, that Hudson's bay has a communication with the ocean, besides that which has been already found out.

Those who have endeavoured to explain these very striking facts, by the supposition of a communication of Hudson's bay with Baffin's bay, or with Davis's straits, are evidently mistaken. They would not scruple to allow it, if they only considered, that the tides

tides are much lower in Davis's ſtraits, and in Baffin's bay, than in Hudſon's.

But if the tides in Hudſon's bay can come neither from the Atlantic ocean, nor from any other northern ſea, in which they are conſtantly much weaker, it follows that they muſt come from ſome part in the ſouth ſea. And this is ſtill further apparent from another leading fact, which is, that the higheſt tides ever obſerved upon theſe coaſts are always occaſioned by the north-weſt winds, which blow directly againſt the mouth of the ſtraits.

Having thus determined, as much as the nature of the ſubject will permit, the exiſtence of this paſſage ſo long and ſo vainly wiſhed for, the next point is to find out in what part of the bay it is to be expected. Every thing inclines us to think, that the attempts, hitherto made without either choice or method, ought to be directed towards Welcome-bay, on the weſtern coaſt. Firſt, the bottom of the ſea is found there at the depth of about eleven fathom; which is an evident ſign that the water comes from ſome ocean, as ſuch a tranſparency is incompatible either with the waters diſcharged from rivers, or with melted ſnow or rain. Secondly, the current keeps this place always free from ice, whilſt all the reſt of the bay is covered with it; and their violence cannot be accounted for but by fuppofing them to come from fome weftern fea. Laftly, the whales, who towards autumn always go in fearch of the warmeft climates, are found in great abundance in thefe parts towards the end of fummer; which would feem to indicate, that they have a way of going from thence to the fouth feas, not to the northern ocean.

It is probable, that the paffage is very fhort. All the rivers that empty themfelves into the weftern coaft of Hudfon's bay are fmall and flow, which feems to prove that they do not come from afar; and that confequently the lands which part the two feas are of a fmall extent. This argument is ftrengthened by the height and regularity of the tides. Wherever there is no other difference between the times of the ebb and flow, but that which is occafioned by the retarded progreffion of the moon in her return to the meridian, it is a certain fign that the ocean from whence thofe tides come is very near. If the paffage is fhort, and not very far to the north, as every thing feems to promife, we may alfo prefume that it is not very difficult. The rapidity of the currents obfervable in thefe latitudes, which do not allow any cakes of ice to continue in them, cannot but give fome weight to this conjecture.

The difcoveries that ftill remain to be made are of fo much importance, that it would

would be folly to give them up. If the paſſage ſo long ſought for were once found, communications would be opened between parts of the globe which hitherto ſeem to have been ſeparated by nature from each other. They would ſoon be extended to the continent of the ſouth ſeas, and to all the numerous iſlands ſcattered upon that immenſe ocean. The intercourſe which has ſubſiſted nearly for three centuries between the commercial nations of Europe and the moſt remote parts of India, being happily freed from the inconveniences of a long navigation, would be much briſker, more conſtant, and more advantageous. It is not to be doubted that the Engliſh would be deſirous of ſecuring an excluſive enjoyment of the fruits of their activity and expences. This wiſh would certainly be very natural, and would be very powerfully ſupported. But as the advantages obtained would be of ſuch a nature, that it would be impoſſible always to preſerve the ſole poſſeſſion of it, we may venture to foretel, that all nations muſt in time become partakers of it with them. Whenever this happens, both the ſtraits of Magellan and Cape Horn will be entirely deſerted, and the Cape of Good Hope much leſs frequented. Whatever the conſequences of the diſcovery may be, it is equally for the intereſt and dignity of Great Britain to purſue

sue her attempts, till they are either crowned with success, or the impossibility of succeeding is fully demonstrated. The resolution she has already taken in 1745 of promising a considerable reward to the seamen who shall make this important discovery, though it be an equal proof of the wisdom and generosity of her councils, is not alone sufficient to attain the end supposed. The English ministry cannot be ignorant, that all the efforts made either by government, or individuals, will prove abortive, till such time as the trade to Hudson's bay shall be entirely free. The company in whose hands it has been ever since 1670, not content with neglecting the chief object of its institution, by taking no steps itself for the discovery of the North-west passage, has thrown every impediment in the way of those who from love of fame, or other motives, have been prompted to this great undertaking. Nothing can ever alter this iniquitous spirit, for it is the very spirit of monopoly.

CHAP. II.
Of NEWFOUNDLAND.

1. *Description.*

HAPPILY the exclusive privilege which prevails at Hudson's bay, and seems to
ex-

exclude all nations from the means of acquiring knowledge and riches, does not extend its oppreſſion to Newfoundland. This iſland, ſituated between 46 and 52 degrees of north latitude, is ſeparated from the coaſt of Labrador only by a channel of moderate breadth, known by the name of Belleiſle Straits. It is of a triangular form, and a little more than three hundred leagues in circumference. We can only ſpeak by conjecture of the inland parts of it, from the difficulty of penetrating far into it, and the apparent inutility of ſucceeding in the attempt. The little that is known of this ſtrait is, that it is full of very ſteep rocks, mountains covered with bad wood, and ſome very narrow and ſandy valleys. Theſe inacceſſible places are ſtocked with deer, which multiply with the greater eaſe, from the ſecurity of their ſituation. No ſavages have ever been ſeen there except ſome Eſquimaux, who come over from the continent in the hunting ſeaſon. The coaſt abounds with creeks, roads, and harbours; is ſometimes covered with moſs, but more commonly with ſmall pebbles, which ſeem as if they had been placed there with deſign, for the purpoſe of drying the fiſh caught in the neighbourhood. In all the open places, where the flat ſtones reflect the ſun's rays, the heat is exceſſive. The reſt of the country is intenſely cold; leſs ſo,

how-

however, from its situation, than from the heights, the forests, the winds, and above all the vast mountains of ice which come out of the northern seas, and are stopped on these coasts. The sky towards the north and western parts is constantly serene; it is much less so towards the east and south, both of them being too near the great bank, which is enveloped in a perpetual fog.

This island was originally discovered in 1497, by the Venetian Cabot, at that time in the service of England, who made no settlement there. It was presumed, from the several voyages made after this, with a view of examining what advantages might be derived from it, that it was fit for nothing but the cod fishery, which is very common in that sea. Accordingly the English used to send out at first small vessels in the spring, which returned again in autumn with their freight of fish both salt and fresh. The consumption of this article became almost universal, and there was a great demand for it particularly among the Roman Catholics. The English availed themselves of this superstition, to enrich themselves at the expence of the clergy, who had formerly drawn their wealth from England; and thought of forming settlements there. The first, that were established at great intervals from one another, were unsuccessful, and were all forsaken faken foon after they were founded. The firſt that acquired any confiſtence was in 1608; the fuccefs of which raifed fuch a fpirit of emulation, that, within forty years, all the fpace between Conception-bay and Cape Ras was peopled by a colony amounting to above four thoufand fouls. Thofe who were employed in the fifhery, being forced, both from the nature of their occupations and that of the foil, to live at a diſtance from each other, cut paths of communication through the woods. Their general rendezvous was at St John's ; where, in an excellent harbour, protected by two mountains at a very fmall diſtance from each other, and large enough to contain above two hundred fhips, they ufed to meet with privateers from the mother country, who carried off the produce of their fifhery, and gave them other neceſſaries in exchange for it.

The French did not wait for this profperity of the Engliſh trade, to turn their thoughts to Newfoundland. They had for a long time frequented the fouthern parts of the ifland, where the Malouins in particular came every year to a place they had called the Petit Nord. After this fome of them fixed without any order upon the coaſt from Cape Ray to Chapeau Rouge; and at length they became numerous enough to form fomething like a town in the bay of Placentia, where
they

they had every convenience that could make their fishery succefsful.

Before the bay is a road of about a league and a half in breadth; not, however, sufficiently sheltered from the N. N. W. winds, which blow there with extreme violence. The strait which forms the entrance of the bay is so confined by rocks, that only one vessel can enter at a time, and even that must be towed in. The bay itself is about eighteen leagues long, and at the extremity of it there is an exceeding safe harbour which holds 150 ships. Notwithstanding the advantage of such a situation for securing to France the whole fishery of the southern coast of Newfoundland, the ministry of Versailles paid very little attention to it. It was not till 1687 that a small fort was built at the mouth of the strait, in which a garrison was placed of about fifty men.

Till this period, the inhabitants whom necefsity had fixed upon this barren and savage coast had been happily forgotten; but from that time began a system of oppression which continued increasing every day from the rapacioufnefs of the successive governors. This tyranny, by which the colonists were prevented from acquiring that degree of competency that was necessary to enable them to pursue their labours with success, must also hinder them from increasing their
num-

numbers. The French fishery, therefore, could never prosper as that of the English. Notwithstanding this, Great Britain did not forget, at the treaty of Utrecht, the inroads that had so often been made upon their territories by their enterprizing neighbours, who, supported by the Canadians accustomed to expeditions and to the fatigues of the chace, trained up in the art of bush-fighting, and exercised in sudden attacks, had several times carried devastation into her settlements. This was sufficient to induce her to demand the entire possession of the island, and the misfortunes of the times obliged the French to submit to this sacrifice; not, however, without reserving to themselves the right of fishing not only on one part of the island, but also on the Great Bank, which was considered as belonging to it.

2. *Fisheries.*

The fish which makes these latitudes so famous, is the cod. They are never above three feet long, and often less; but there are no fish in the whole ocean whose mouth is so large in proportion to their size, or which are so voracious. Broken pieces of earthen ware, iron, and glass, are often found in their bellies. The stomach, indeed, does not digest these hard substances, as it hath long
been

been thought; but it hath the power of inverting itself, like a pocket, and thus discharges whatever loads it.

The cod fish is found in the northern seas of Europe. The fishery is carried on by thirty English, sixty French, and 150 Dutch vessels, one with another from 80 to 100 tons burden. Their competitors are the Irish, and especially the Norwegians. The latter are employed, before the fishing season, in collecting upon the coast the eggs of the cod, which is a bait necessary to catch pilchards. They sell, *communibus annis*, from twenty to twenty-two thousand tons of this fish, at 7 s. $10\frac{1}{2}$ d. per ton. If it could be disposed of, a great deal more would be caught; for an able naturalist, who has had the patience to count the eggs of one single cod, has found 9,344,000 of them. This profusion of nature must still be increased at Newfoundland, where the cod fish is found in infinitely greater plenty.

The fish of Newfoundland is also more delicate, though not so white; but it is not an object of trade when fresh, and only serves for the food of those who are employed on the fishery. When it is salted and dried, or only salted, it becomes an useful article to a great part of Europe and America. That which is only salted is called green cod, and is caught upon the great bank.

This flip of land is one of those mountains formed under water by the earth which the sea is continually washing away from the continent. Both its extremities terminate so much in a point, that it is difficult to assign the precise extent of it; but it is generally reckoned to be 160 leagues long and 90 broad. Towards the middle of it, on the European side, is a kind of bay, which has been called the Ditch. Throughout all this space, the depth of water is very different; in some places there are only five, in others above sixty fathom. The sun scarce ever shews itself there, and the sky is generally covered with a thick cold fog. The waves are always agitated, and the winds always impetuous around it, which must be owing to the sea being irregularly driven forward by currents, which bear sometimes on one side, sometimes on the other, and strike against the borders, which are every where perpendicular, and repel them with equal violence. This is most likely to be the true cause; because on the bank itself, at some distance from the coast, it is as quiet as in a bay, except when there happens to be a forced wind which comes from a greater distance.

From the middle of July to the latter end of August there is no cod found either upon the great bank or any of the small ones near it; but all the rest of the year the fishery is carried on. The ſhips employed in it are commonly from 50 to 150 tons, and carry not leſs than twelve or more than twenty-five men aboard. Theſe fiſhermen are provided with lines; and before they ſet to work, catch a fiſh called the caplin, which is a bait for the cod.

Previous to their entering upon the fiſhery, they build a gallery on the outſide of the ſhip, which reaches from the main maſt to the ſtern, and ſometimes the whole length of it. This gallery is furniſhed with barrels, of which the top is beaten out. The fiſhermen place themſelves within theſe, and are ſheltered from the weather by a pitched covering faſtened to the barrels. As ſoon as they catch a cod, they cut out its tongue, and give it to one of the boys to carry to a perſon appointed for the purpoſe, who immediately ſtrikes off the head, plucks out the liver and entrails, and then lets it fall thro' a ſmall hatchway between the decks; when another man takes it, and draws out the bone as far as the navel, and then lets it ſink through another hatchway into the hold; where it is ſalted and ranged in piles. The perſon who ſalts it, is attentive to leave ſalt enough between the rows of fiſh which form the piles, to prevent their touching each other, and yet not to leave too much, as either exceſs would ſpoil the cod.

In

In the right of nature, the fishing upon the great bank ought to have been common to all mankind: notwithstanding which, the two powers who have colonies in North America have made very little difficulty of appropriating it to themselves; and Spain, who alone could have any claim to it, and who from the number of her monks might have pleaded the necessity of asserting it, entirely gave up the matter at the last peace; since which time the English and French are the only nations who frequent these latitudes.

In 1768, France set out 145 ships; the expence of which is valued at 111,431 *l.* 5 *s.* These vessels, which carried in all 8830 tons, were manned by 1700 men; who upon an average, and according to calculations ascertained by being often repeated, must have caught each 700 fish; so that the whole of the fishery must have produced 1,190,000.

These cod are divided into three separate classes; the first consists of those which are twenty-four inches in length or upwards, the second comprehends those which measure from nineteen to twenty-four, and the third takes in all that are under nineteen inches. If the fishery has yielded, as it commonly does, two fifths of good fish, two fifths of moderate fish, and one fifth of bad, and if the fish has been sold at the common price,

F 2 which

which is 6*l*. 11*s*. 3*d*. the hundred weight, the produce of the whole fishery will amount to 45,937*l*. 10*s*. The hundred weight is composed of 136 cod of the first quality, and of 272 of the second; which two sorts taken together sell for 7*l*. 17*s*. 6*d*. the hundred. Only 136 cod are required to make up the hundred weight of the third class; but this hundred weight sells only for one third of the other, and is worth only 2*l*. 12*s*. 6*d*. when the first is worth 7*l*. 17*s*. 6*d*. Consequently the 1,190,000 cod really caught, and reduced in this manner, make only 700,000 cod, which at 6*l*. 11*s*. 3*d*. the hundred weight, which is the mean price of the three sorts of fish, will produce only 45,937*l*. 10*s*. Out of this the crew must receive for their share, which is one fifth, 9,187*l*. 10*s*. Consequently there remains only 36,750*l*. profit for the undertakers. This is not sufficient, as will be easily be made evident. First, we must deduct the expences of unloading; which, for the 145 ships, cannot be reckoned at less than 380*l*. 12*s*. 6*d*. The insurance of 111,431*l*. 5*s*. at five per cent. must amount to 5,571*l*. 11*s*. 3*d*. As much also must be deducted for the interest of the money. The value of the ships must be estimated at two thirds of the capital advanced, and will therefore be 74,287*l*. 10*s*. If we allow no more than five per cent. for the annual repair of the

the ſhips, we ſhall ſtill be obliged to ſubtract 3,714 *l.* 7 *s.* 6 *d.* from the profits. All theſe ſums added together make a loſs of 15,631 *l.* 17 *s.* 6 *d.* which being aſſeſſed upon a capital of 111,431 *l.* 5 *s.* amounts to a loſs of 12 *s.* 3 *d.* farthing per cent.

The French miniſtry muſt, therefore, either abſolutely give up the fiſhery of the green cod, which is conſumed in the capital, and in the northern provinces of France, or muſt take off the enormous duties which are at preſent impoſed upon this kind of conſumption. If they delay much longer to ſacrifice this inſignificant portion of the public revenue to ſo valuable a branch of trade, they will ſoon have the mortification to ſee the revenue diſappear with the trade that produced it. The habit of trading, the hopes of amendment, the averſion the traders have for ſelling their ſhips and ſtock under prime coſt; theſe are the only motives that induce them ſtill to continue the cod fiſhery: motives which muſt certainly have an end; and, if we may judge from the general appearance of diſſatisfaction, that end is not very far off.

The Engliſh, the produce of whoſe fiſhery is ſubject to no tax, have not the ſame reaſons for giving it up. They have alſo another advantage; which is, that not coming from Europe, as their competitors do, but only from Newfoundland or other places almoſt as near, they can make uſe of very ſmall veſſels, which are eaſily managed, are not much raiſed above the water, and where ſails may be brought level with the deck, ſo that being little expoſed, even to the moſt violent winds, their work is ſeldom interrupted by the roughneſs of the weather. Beſides, they do not, as other ſeamen, loſe their time in procuring baits, which they bring along with them. In a word, their ſailors are more inured to the fatigues, more accuſtomed to the cold, and more ready at the buſineſs.

The Engliſh, however, attend very little to the fiſhery of the great cod; becauſe they have no mart for diſpoſing of it. In this branch they do not ſell half ſo much as their rivals. As their cod is prepared with very little care, they ſeldom make up a complete cargo of it. For fear of its ſpoiling, they commonly quit the Great Bank, with two thirds and very often with not more than half their lading, which they ſell to the Spaniſh and Portugueſe, and amongſt their own countrymen. But they make themſelves amends for this trifling exportation of the green cod, by the great ſuperiority they have acquired in all markets for the dry cod.

This branch of trade is carried on in two different ways. That which is called the Wandering Fiſhery, belongs to veſſels which ſail every year from Europe to Newfoundland,

land, at the end of March, or in April. As they come near the island, they frequently meet with a quantity of ice, which the northern currents push towards the south, which is broken to pieces by repeated shocks, and melts sooner or later at the return of the heats. These cakes of ice are frequently a league in circumference; they are as high as the loftiest mountains, and reach to above sixty or eighty fathoms under water. When they are joined to lesser pieces, they sometimes occupy a space of a hundred leagues in length, and twenty-five or thirty in breadth. Interest, which obliges the mariners to come to their landings as soon as possible, that they may chuse the harbours most favourable to the fishery, makes them brave the rigour of the seasons and of the elements, which all conspire against human industry. Neither the most formidable rampart erected by military art, nor the dreadful cannonade of a besieged town, nor the terrors of the most skilful and obstinate sea-fight, require so much intrepidity and experience to encounter, as do these enormous floating bulwarks which the sea opposes to these small fleets of fishermen. But the most insatiable of all passions, the thirst of gold, surmounts every obstacle, and carries the mariner across these mountains of ice to the spot where the ships are to take in their lading.

The firft thing to be done after landing is to cut wood and erect fcaffolds. Thefe labours employ every body. When they are finifhed, the company divide: one half of the crew ftays afhore to cure the fifh; and the other goes on board in fmall boats, with three men in thofe which are intended for the fifhery of the caplin, and four for the cod. Thefe laft, which are the moft numerous, fail before it is light, generally at the diftance of three, four, or five leagues from the coaft, and return in the evening to the fcaffolds near the fea-fide, where they depofite the produce of the day.

When one man has taken off the cod's head and emptied the body, he gives it to another, who flices it and puts in falt, where it is left till it is quite dry. It is then heaped up in piles, and left for fome days to exfude. It is then again laid on the ftrand, where it continues drying, and takes the colour we fee it have in Europe.

There are no fatigues whatever to be compared with the labours of this fifhery, which hardly leave thofe who work at it four hours reft in the night. Happily, the falubrity of the climate keeps up the health of the people againft fuch fevere trials; and thefe labours would be thought nothing of, if they were rewarded by the produce.

But there are fome harbours where the
ftrand

strand is at so great a distance from the sea, that a great deal of time is lost in getting to them; and others, in which the bottom is of solid rock, and without varech, so that the fish do not frequent them. There are others again, where the fish grow yellow from a mixture of fresh water with the salt; and some, in which it is burned up by the reverberation of the sun's rays reflected from the mountains. Even in the most favourable harbours, the people are not always sure of a succesful fishery. The fish cannot abound equally in all parts; it is sometimes found to the north, sometimes to the south, and at other times in the middle of the coast, according as it is driven by the winds or attracted by the caplin. The fishermen, who happen to fix at a distance from the places which the fish may chuse to frequent, are very unfortunate; for their expences are all thrown away by the impossibility of following the fish with all that is requisite for the fishery.

The fishery ends about the beginning of September, because at that time the sun is no longer powerful enough to dry the fish; but when it has been succesful, the managers give over before that time, and make the best of their way either to the Caribbees, or to the Roman Catholic states in Europe, that they may not be deprived of the advantages

tages of the first market, which might be lost by an over stock.

In 1768, France sent out in this trade 114 vessels, carrying in all 15,590 tons; the prime cost of which, together with the first expences of setting out, had amounted to 247,668*l*. 15*s*. The united crews, half of which were employed in taking the fish, and the other half in curing it, consisted of 8022 men. Every fisherman must have taken for his share 6000 cod, and consequently the produce of the whole must have been 24,066,000 cod. Experience shews that there are 125 cod to each quintal. Consequently 24,066,000 must have made 162,528 quintals. Each quintal upon an average sold at about 14*s*. 5*d*. which makes, for the whole sale 138,875*l*. 17*s*. 2¼*d*. As every hundred quintal of cod yields one barrel of oil, 192,528 quintals must have yielded 1925 barrels, which at 5*l*. 5*s*. a barrel makes 10,106*l*. 5*s*. Add to these, the profits of freight made by the ships in returning home from the ports where they sold their cargoes, which are estimated at 8662*l*. 10*s*. and the total profits of the fishery will not be found to have amounted to more than 157,644*l*. 12*s*. 2¼*d*.

We may spare our readers a detail of the expences of unloading, which are as troublesome in their minuteness as in their insignificancy. The calculations of these have been made

made with the greatest care and attention, and the accounts confirmed by very intelligent and disinterested men, who from their professions must have been the proper judges of this matter. They amount in the whole to 30,436 *l.* 10 *s.* 9 *d.* so that the net produce of the fishery amounted only to 127,208 *l.* 11 *s.* $3\frac{1}{2}$ *d.*

From these profits the insurance-money must be deducted, which at 6 per cent. upon a capital of 247,668 *l.* 15 *s.* amounts to 14,860 *l.* 2 *s.* 6 *d.* We must also reckon the interest of the money; making, at 5 per cent. 12,383 *l.* 8 *s.* 9 *d.* Neither must we omit the wear of the ships; the prime cost of which, making half the whole capital, must be set down at 123,834 *l.* 7 *s.* 6 *d.* This wear therefore, which cannot be reckoned at less than 6 per cent. must amount to 6191 *l.* 14 *s.* $4\frac{1}{2}$ *d.* Admitting all these circumstances, which indeed cannot be called in question, it follows that the French have lost upon this fishery, in 1768, 30,061 *l.* 1 *s.* 8 *d.* and consequently 10 *s.* $7\frac{1}{8}$ *d.* per cent. of their capital.

Such losses, which unfortunately have been but too often repeated, will wean the nation more and more from this ruinous branch of trade. Individuals who still carry it on, will soon give it up; and it is even probable, that, in imitation of the English, they would have done so already, if like them they had been

able

able to make themselves amends by the stationary fishery.

By Stationary Fishery, we are to understand that which is made by the Europeans who have settlements on those coasts of America where the cod is most plentiful. It is infinitely more profitable than the wandering fishery, because it requires much less expence, and may be continued much longer. These advantages the French enjoyed as long as they remained peaceable possessors of Acadia, Cape Breton, Canada, and part of Newfoundland. They have lost them one after another by the errors of government; and, from the wreck of these riches, have only preserved a right of salting and drying their fish to the north of Newfoundland, from Cape Bona Vista to Point Rich. All the fixed establishments left by the peace of 1763, are reduced to the island of St Peters, and the two islands of Miquelon, which they are not even at liberty to build fortifications upon. There are 800 inhabitants at St Peters, not more than one hundred at great Miquelon, and only one family on the smaller. The fishery, which is extremely convenient upon the two first, is entirely impracticable on the lesser island; but this last supplies them both with wood, and particularly St Peters, which had none of its own. Nature, however, has made amends for this deficiency at St Peters, by by an excellent harbour, which indeed is the only one in this small archipelago. In 1768, they took 24,390 quintals of cod: but this quantity will not much increase; because the English not only refuse the French the liberty of fishing in the narrow channel which separates these islands from the southern coasts of Newfoundland, but have even seized some of the sloops which attempted it.

This severity, which is not warranted by treaty, and only maintained by force, is rendered still more odious by the extensiveness of their own possessions, which reach to all the islands where the fish is to be found. Their principal settlement is at Newfoundland, where there are about 8000 English, who are all employed in the fishery. No more than nine or ten ships a-year are sent out from the mother country for this purpose; and there are some few more which engage in other articles of commerce; but the greater part only exchange the productions of Europe for fish, or carry off the fruit of the industry of the inhabitants.

Before 1755, the fisheries of the two rival nations were nearly equal, from their own accounts; with this difference only, that France, on account of its population and religion, consumed more at home, and sold less: but since she has lost her possessions in North America, one year with another, the two fisheries, that is the Stationary and the Wandering, united, have not yielded more than 216,918 quintals of dry cod; which is barely sufficient for the consumption of its southern provinces at home, and of course admits of no exportation to the colonies.

It may be asserted, that the rival nation, on the contrary, has increased its fishery two thirds since its conquests, making in all 651,115 quintals; the profits of which, valuing each quintal at no more than 12 *s*. 3 *d*. a difference owing to its being cured with less care than the French fish, will amount to 398,807 *l*. 6 *s*. 6 *d*. One fourth of this is sufficient for the consumption of Great Britain and her colonies; consequently what is sold in Spain, Portugal, and all the sugar-islands, amounts to a sum of 299,105 *l*. 9 *s*. 10½ *d*. returned to the mother country either in specie or commodities. This object of exportation would have been still more considerable, if, when the court of London made the conquest of Cape Breton and St John's, they had not been so inhuman as to drive out the French whom they found settled there; who have never yet been replaced, and probably never will be. The same bad policy has also been followed in Nova Scotia.

CHAP.

CHAP. III.

Of Nova Scotia.

1. *The French give it up to England, after having been a long time in poſſeſſion of it themſelves.*

Nova Scotia, by which is at preſent to be underſtood all the coaſt of 300 leagues in length contained between the limits of New England and the ſouth coaſt of the river St Lawrence, ſeemed at firſt to have comprehended only the great triangular peninſula lying nearly in the middle of this ſpace. This peninſula, which the French called Acadie, is extremely well ſituated for the ſhips which come from the Caribbees to water at. It offers them a great number of excellent ports in which ſhips may enter and go out of with all winds. There is a great quantity of cod upon the coaſt, and ſtill more upon ſmall banks at the diſtance of a few leagues. The ſoil, which is very gravelly, is extremely convenient for drying the cod: it abounds beſides with good wood, and land fit for ſeveral ſorts of cultivation, and extremely well ſituated for the fur trade of the neighbouring continent. Tho' this climate is in the temperate zone, the winters are long and severe; and they are followed by sudden and excessive heats, to which generally succeed very thick fogs, which last a long time. These circumstances make this rather a disagreeable country, though it cannot be reckoned an unwholesome one.

It was in 1604 that the French settled in Acadie, four years before they had built the smallest hut in Canada. Instead of fixing towards the east of the peninsula, where they would have had larger seas, an easy navigation, and plenty of cod, they chose a small bay, afterwards called the French bay, which had none of these advantages. It has been said, that they were induced by the beauty of Port-Royal, where a thousand ships may ride in safety from every wind, where there is an excellent bottom, and at all times four or five fathom of water, and eighteen at the entrance. It is most probable that the founders of this colony were led to chuse this situation, from its vicinity to the countries abounding in furs, of which the exclusive trade had been granted to them. This conjecture is confirmed by the following circumstance: That both the first monopolizers, and those who succeeded them, took the utmost pains to divert the attention of their countrymen, whom restlessness or necessity brought into these regions, from the clearing of the woods, the breeding of cattle, from fishing, and from every kind of culture; chusing rather to engage the industry of these adventurers in hunting, or in trading with the savages.

The mischiefs arising from a false system of administration at length discovered the fatal effects of exclusive charters. It would be an insult to the truth and dignity of history to say that this happened in France from any attention to the common rights of the nation, at a time when these rights were most openly violated. This sacred tie, which alone can secure the safety of the people, while it gives a sanction to the power of kings, was never known in France. But in the most absolute government a spirit of ambition sometimes affects what in equitable and moderate ones is done from principles of justice. The ministers of Lewis XIV. who wished to make their master respectable that they might reflect some dignity on themselves, perceived that they should not succeed without the support of riches; and that a people to whom nature has not given any mines, cannot acquire wealth but by agriculture and commerce. Both these resources had been hitherto choked up in the colonies by the restraints laid upon all things from an improper interference. These impediments were at last removed; but Acadia either knew not how, or was not able, to make use of this liberty.

This colony was yet in its infancy, when the settlement which has since become so famous under the name of New-England was first made in its neighbourhood. The rapid success of the cultures in this new colony did not much attract the notice of the French. This kind of prosperity did not excite any jealousy between the two nations. But when they began to suspect that there was likely to be a competition for the beaver trade and furs, they endeavoured to secure to themselves the sole property of it; and they were unfortunate enough to succeed.

At their first arrival in Acadia, they had found the peninsula, as well as the forests of the neighbouring continent, peopled with small nations of savages who went under the general name of Abenakies. Though equally fond of war as other savage nations, they were, however, more sociable in their manners. The missionaries, easily insinuating themselves amongst them, had so far inculcated their tenets, as to make enthusiasts of them. At the same time that they taught them their religion, they inspired them with that hatred which they themselves entertained for the English name. This fundamental article of their new worship, being that which most exerted its influence on their senses, and the only

only one that favoured their paffion for war; they adopted it with all the rage that was natural to them. They not only refufed to make any exchange with the Englifh, but alfo frequently attacked and plundered their fettlements. Their attacks became more frequent, more obftinate, and more regular, fince they had chofen St Cafteins, formerly captain of the regiment of Carignan, for their commander; he having fettled among them, married one of their women, and conforming in every refpect to their mode of life.

When the Englifh faw that all efforts either to reconcile the favages, or to deftroy them in their forefts, were ineffectual, they fell upon Acadia, which they looked upon with reafon as the only caufe of all thefe calamities. Whenever the leaft hoftility took place between the two mother countries, the peninfula was attacked. Having no defence from Canada, from which it was too far diftant, and very little from Port-royal, which was only furrounded by a few weak pallifadoes, it was conftantly taken. It undoubtedly afforded fome fatisfaction to the New-Englanders to ravage this colony, and to retard its progrefs; but ftill this was not fufficient to difpel the fufpicions excited by a nation almoft more formidable by what fhe is able to do, than by what fhe really does. Obliged as they were, however unwillingly, to restore their conquest at each treaty of peace, they waited with impatience till Great Britain should acquire such a superiority as would enable her to dispense with this restitution. The end of the war on account of the Spanish succession brought on the decisive moment; and the court of Versailles was for ever deprived of a possession of which it had never known the importance.

The ardour which the English had shewn for the possession of this territory did not manifest itself afterwards in the care they took to maintain or to improve it. Having built a very slight fortification at Port-royal, which had taken the name of Annapolis in honour of Queen Anne, they contented themselves with putting a very small garrison in it. The indifference shewn by the government infected the nation, a circumstance not usual in a free country. Not more than five English families came over to Acadia, which still remained inhabited by the first colonists; who were only persuaded to stay upon a promise made them of never being compelled to bear arms against their ancient country. Such was the attachment which the French then had for the honour of their country. Cherished by the government, respected by foreign nations, and attached to their king by a series of prosperities which had rendered them illustrious, and aggrandized

dized them, they were infpired with that fpirit of patriotifm which arifes from fuccefs. They confidered it as glorious to bear the name of Frenchmen, and could not think of foregoing the title. The Acadians, therefore, who, in fubmitting to a new yoke, had fworn never to bear arms againft their former ftandards, were called the French Neutrals.

There were twelve or thirteen hundred of them fettled in the capital, the reft were difperfed in the neighbouring country. No magiftrate was ever fet over them; and they were never acquainted with the laws of England. No rents or taxes of any kind were ever exacted from them. Their new fovereign feemed to have forgotten them; and he himfelf was a total ftranger to them.

2. *Manners of the French who remained fubject to the Englifh government in Nova Scotia.*

HUNTING and fifhing, which had formerly been the delight of the colony, and might have ftill fupplied it with fubfiftence, had no further attraction for a fimple and quiet people, and gave way to agriculture. It had been eftablifhed in the marfhes and the low lands by repelling the fea and rivers, which covered thefe plains, with dikes.

These grounds yielded fifty for one at first, and afterwards fifteen or twenty for one at least. Wheat and oats succeeded best in them; but they likewise produced rye, barley, and maize. There were also potatoes in great plenty, the use of which was become common.

At the same time the immense meadows were covered with numerous flocks. They computed as much as sixty thousand head of horned cattle; and most families had several horses, though the tillage was carried on by oxen. The habitations, built all of wood, were extremely convenient, and furnished as neatly as a substantial farmer's house in Europe. They bred a great deal of poultry of all kinds, which made a variety in their food for the most part wholesome and plentiful. Their common drink was beer and cyder, to which they sometimes added rum. Their usual clothing was in general the produce of their own flax, or the fleeces of their own sheep. With these they made common linens and coarse cloths. If any of them had a desire for articles of greater luxury, they drew them from Annapolis or Louisbourg, and gave in exchange corn, cattle, or furs.

The neutral French had nothing else to give their neighbours, and made still fewer exchanges among themselves, because each separate family was able and had been
used

used to provide for its own wants. They, therefore, knew nothing of paper-currency, which was so common throughout the rest of North America. Even the small quantity of specie which had slipped into the colony did not inspire that activity in which consists its real value.

Their manners were of course extremely simple. There never was a cause, either civil or criminal, of importance enough to be carried before the court of judicature established at Annapolis. Whatever little differences arose from time to time among them were amicably adjusted by their elders. All their public acts were drawn by their pastors, who had likewise the keeping of their wills, for which and their religious services the inhabitants paid a twenty-seventh part of their harvest.

These were always plentiful enough to afford more means than there were objects for generosity. Real misery was entirely unknown, and benevolence prevented the demands of poverty. Every misfortune was relieved, as it were, before it could be felt, without ostentation on the one hand, and without meanness on the other. It was in short a society of brethren, every individual of which was equally ready to give and to receive what he thought the common right of mankind.

So perfect a harmony naturally prevented all those connections of gallantry which are so often fatal to the peace of families. There never was an instance in this society of an unlawful commerce between the two sexes. This evil was prevented by early marriages; for no one passed his youth in a state of celibacy. As soon as a young man came to the proper age, the community built him a house, broke up the lands about it, sowed them, and supplied them with all the necessaries of life for a twelvemonth. Here he received the partner whom he had chosen, and who brought him her portion in flocks. This new family grew and prospered like the others. In 1749, all together made a population of eighteen thousand souls.

At this period Great Britain perceived of what consequence the possession of Acadia might be to her commerce. The peace, which necessarily left a great number of men without employment, furnished an opportunity, by the disbanding of the troops, for peopling and cultivating a vast and fertile territory. The British ministry offered particular advantages to all who would go over and settle in Acadia. Every soldier, sailor, and workman, was to have fifty acres of land himself, and ten for every person he carried over in his family. All non-commissioned officers were allowed eighty for themselves,

and

and fifty for their wives and children; enfigns, 200; lieutenants, 300; captains, 460; and all officers of a higher rank, 600; together with thirty for each of their dependents. The land was to be tax-free for the firſt ten years, and never to pay above one ſhilling for fifty acres. Beſides this, the government engaged to advance or reimburſe the expences of paſſage, to build houſes, to furniſh all the neceſſary inſtruments for fiſhery or agriculture, and to defray the expences of ſubſiſtence for the firſt year. Theſe encouragements determined three thouſand ſeven hundred and fifty perſons, in the month of May 1749, to go to America, rather than run the riſk of ſtarving in Europe.

The new colony was intended to form an eſtabliſhment to the ſouth-eaſt of Acadia, in a place which the ſavages had formerly called Chebucto, and the Engliſh Halifax. This ſituation was preferred to ſeveral others where the ſoil was better, for the ſake of eſtabliſhing in its neighbourhood an excellent cod fiſhery, and fortifying one of the fineſt harbours in America. But as it was the ſpot moſt favourable for the chace, the Engliſh were obliged to diſpute it with the Micmac Indians, who moſtly frequented it. Theſe ſavages defended with obſtinacy a territory they held from nature; and it was not till after very great loſſes that the Engliſh
drove

drove them out from their possessions.

This war was not entirely finished, when there was some agitation discovered among the neutral French. A people, whose manners were so simple, and who enjoyed such liberty, could not but perceive that it was impossible there should be any serious thoughts in settling in countries so near to them without their independence being affected by it. To this apprehension was added that of seeing their religion in danger. Their priests, either heated by their own enthusiasm, or secretly instigated by the governors of Canada, persuaded them to credit every thing they chose to suggest against the English, whom they called Heretics. This word, which has so powerful an influence on deluded minds, determined this happy American colony to quit their habitations and remove to New France, where they were offered lands. This resolution many of them executed immediately, without considering the consequences of it; the rest were preparing to follow, as soon as they had provided for their safety. The English government, either from policy or caprice, determined to prevent them by an act of treachery, always base and cruel in those to whom power affords milder methods. Under a pretence of exacting a renewal of the oath which they had taken at the time of their becoming English subjects, they

they assembled those together who were not yet gone; and when they had collected them, immediately embarked them on board of ships, which transported them to the other English colonies, where the greater part of them died of grief and vexation rather than want.

Such are the fruits of national jealousies, of that rapaciousness inherent to all governments which incessantly preys both upon mankind and upon land! What an enemy loses is reckoned a gain; what he gains, is looked upon as a loss. When a town cannot be taken, it is starved; when it cannot be maintained, it is burnt to ashes, or its foundation rased. Rather than surrender, a ship or a fortification is blown up by powder and by mines. A despotic government separates its enemies from its slaves by immense deserts, to prevent the eruptions of the one and the emigrations of the other.

Thus Spain chose rather to make a wilderness of her own country, and a grave of America, than to divide its riches with any other of the European nations. The Dutch have been guilty of every public and private crime to deprive other commercial nations of the spice-trade. They have oftentimes even thrown whole cargoes into the sea, rather than they would sell them at a low price. France rather chose to give up Louisiana to the

the Spaniards, than to let it fall into the hands of the English; and England destroyed the French vessels, to prevent their returning to France. Can we assert, after this, that policy and society were instituted for the happiness of mankind? Yes, they were instituted to screen the wicked man, and to secure the man in power.

3. *Present state of Nova Scotia.*

SINCE the emigration of a people who owed their happiness to their virtuous obscurity, Nova Scotia has been but thinly inhabited. It seems as if the envy that depopulated the country had blasted it. At least the punishment of the injustice falls upon the authors of it; for there is not a single inhabitant to be seen upon all that length of coast between the river St Lawrence and the peninsula; nor do the rocks, the sands, and marshes, with which it is at present covered, make it probable that it ever will be peopled. The cod, indeed, which abounds in some of its bays, draws every year a small number of fishermen during the season.

There are only three settlements in the rest of the province. Annapolis, the most ancient of them, waits for fresh inhabitants to take the place of the unhappy Frenchmen who were driven from it; and it seems to pro-

promife them rich returns from the fertility of her foil.

Lunenburgh, the fecond fettlement, was founded a few years ago by 800 Germans come from Halifax. At firft, it did not promife much fuccefs; but it is confiderably improved by the unremitted induftry of that warlike and wife people, who, contented with defending their own territory, feldom go out of it, but to cultivate others which they are not ambitious of conquering. They have fertilized all the countries under the Englifh dominion, wherever chance had conducted them.

Halifax will always continue to be the principal place of the province; an advantage it owes to the encouragements lavifhed upon it by the mother country. Their expences for this fettlement from its firft foundation to the year 1769, amounted to more than 3937*l*. 10*s*. per annum. Such favours were not ill beftowed upon a city, which, from its fituation, is the natural rendezvous of both the land and fea forces which Great Britain fometimes thinks herfelf obliged to maintain in America, as well for the defence of her fifheries and the protection of her fugar-iflands, as for the purpofe of maintaining her connections with her northern colonies. Halifax, indeed, derives more of its fplendor from the motion and activity which

is

is constantly kept up in its ports, than either from its cultivation which is trifling, or from its fisheries which have not been considerably improved, though they consist of cod, mackerel, and the seal. It is not even in the state it should be as a fortified town. The malversations of persons employed, who instead of the fortifications ordered and paid for by the mother country, have only erected a few batteries without any ditch round the city, make it liable to fall without resistance into the hands of the first enemy that attacks it. In 1757, the inhabitants of the county of Halifax rated the value of their houses, cattle, and merchandise, at about 295,312 *l.* 10 *s.* This sum, which makes about two thirds of the riches of the whole province, has not increased above one fourth since that time.

The desire of putting a stop to this state of languor was, probably, one of the motives which induced the British government to constitute a court of admiralty for all North America, and to place the seat of it at Halifax, in 1763. Before this period, the justices of peace used to be the judges of all violations of the act of navigation; but the partiality these magistrates used to shew in their judgments for the colony where they were born and which had chosen them, made their ministry useless, and even prejudicial

to

to the mother country. It was presumed, that if enlightened men were sent from Europe, and well supported, they would impress more respect for their determination. The event has justified this policy. Since that regulation, the commercial laws have been better observed; but still great inconveniences have ensued from the distance of many provinces from the seat of this new tribunal. It is probable, that, to remedy these, administration will be forced to multiply the number of the courts, and disperse them in places convenient for the people to have access to them. Nova Scotia will then lose the temporary advantage it gains from being the resort of those who come for justice; but it will, probably, find out other natural sources of wealth within itself. It has some, indeed, that are peculiar to it. The exceeding fine flax it produces, of which the three kingdoms are so much in want, must hasten the progress of its improvement.

CHAP. IV.

Of NEW ENGLAND.

1. *Foundation.*

NEW ENGLAND, like the mother country, has signalized itself by many acts of violence; and was actuated by the same turbulent

lent spirit. It took its rise in troublesome times, and its infant-state was disturbed with many dreadful commotions. It was discovered in the beginning of the last century, and called North Virginia; but no Europeans settled there till the year 1608. The first colony, which was weak and ill directed, did not succeed; and for some time after, there were only a few adventurers who came over at times in the summer, built themselves temporary huts for the sake of trading with the savages, and like them disappeared again for the rest of the year. Fanaticism, which had depopulated America to the south, was destined to repopulate it in the north. At length some English presbyterians, who had been driven from their own country, and had taken refuge in Holland, that universal asylum of liberty, resolved to found a church for their sect in a new hemisphere. They therefore purchased, in 1621, the charter of the English North Virginia Company: for they were not poor enough to wait in patience till their virtues should have made them prosperous. Forty-one families, making in all 120 persons, set out, guided by enthusiasm, which, whether founded upon error or truth, is always productive of great actions. They landed at the beginning of a very hard winter; and found a country entirely covered with wood, which offered a

very

very melancholy prospect to men already exhausted with the fatigues of their journey. Near one half perished either from the cold, the scurvy, or distress; the rest were kept alive for some time by a spirit of enthusiasm, and the steadiness of character they had contracted under the persecution of episcopal tyranny. But their courage was beginning to fail, when it was revived by the arrival of sixty savage warriors, who came to them in the spring, headed by their chief. Freedom seemed to exult that she had thus brought together from the extremities of the world two such different people; who immediately entered into a reciprocal alliance of friendship and protection. The old tenants assigned for ever to the new ones all the lands in the neighbourhood of the settlement they had formed under the name of New Plymouth; and one of the savages, who understood a little English, staid with them to teach them how to cultivate the maize, and instruct them in the manner of fishing upon their coast.

This kindness enabled the colony to wait for the companions they expected from Europe, with seeds and all sorts of domestic animals. At first they came but slowly; but the persecution of the puritans in England increased the number of proselytes (as is always the case) to such a degree in America, that,

that, in 1630, they were obliged to form different settlements, of which Boston soon became the principal. These first settlers were not merely ecclesiastics, who had been driven out of their preferment for their opinions; nor those sectaries, influenced by new opinions, that are so frequent among the common people. There were among them several persons of high rank, who having embraced puritanism either from motives of caprice, ambition, or even of conscience, had taken the precaution to secure themselves an asylum in these distant regions. They had caused houses to be built, and lands to be cleared, with a view of retiring there, if their endeavours in the cause of civil and religious liberty should prove abortive. The same fanatical spirit that had introduced anarchy into the mother country, kept the colony in a state of subordination; or rather, a severity of manners had the same effect as laws in a savage climate.

The inhabitants of New England lived peaceably for a long time without any regular form of polity. It was not that their charter had not authorised them to establish any mode of government they might chuse; but these enthusiasts were not agreed amongst themselves upon the plan of their republic, and government was not sufficiently concerned about them to urge them to secure their own

own tranquillity. At length they grew senfible of the neceſſity of a regular legiſlation; and this great work, which virtue and genius united have never attempted but with diffidence, was boldly undertaken by blind fanaticiſm. It bore the ſtamp of the rude prejudices on which it had been formed.

There was in this new code a ſingular mixture of good and evil, of wiſdom and folly. No man was allowed to have any ſhare in the government, except he was a member of the eſtabliſhed church. Witchcraft, perjury, blaſphemy, and adultery, were made capital offences; and children were alſo puniſhed with death, either for curſing or ſtriking their parents. On the other hand, marriages were to be ſolemnized by the magiſtrate. The price of corn was fixed at 2 *s.* 11 *d.* halfpenny per buſhel. The ſavages who neglected to cultivate their lands were to be deprived of them by law. Europeans were forbidden under a heavy penalty to ſell them any ſtrong liquors or warlike ſtores. All thoſe who were detected either in lying, or drunkenneſs, or dancing, were ordered to be publicly whipped. But at the ſame time that amuſements were forbidden equally with vices and crimes, one might ſwear by paying a penalty of a ſhilling, and break the ſabbath for three pounds. It was eſteemed an indulgence to be able to atone by money for a neglect of prayer, or for uttering a rash oath. But it is still more extraordinary that the worship of images was forbidden to the puritans on pain of death; which was also inflicted on Roman Catholic priests who should return to the colony after they had been banished, and on Quakers who should appear again after having been whipped, branded, and expelled. Such was the abhorrence for these sectaries, who had themselves an aversion for every kind of cruelty, that whoever either brought one of them into the country, or harboured him but for one hour, was exposed to pay a considerable fine.

2 *Fanaticism occasions great calamities there.*

Those unfortunate members of the colony, who, less violent than their brethren, ventured to deny the coercive power of the magistrate in matters of religion, were persecuted with still greater rigour. This appeared a blasphemy to those divines who had rather chosen to quit their country than to shew any deference to episcopal authority. By that natural tendency of the human heart from the love of independence to that tyranny, they changed their opinions as they changed the climate; and only seemed to arrogate freedom of thought to themselves in order to deny

deny it to others. This system was supported by the severities of the law, which attempted to put a stop to every difference in opinion, by imposing capital punishment on all who dissented. Whoever was either convicted, or even suspected, of entertaining sentiments of toleration, was exposed to such cruel oppressions, that they were forced to fly from their first asylum, and seek refuge in another. They found one on the same continent; and as New England had been first founded by persecution, its limits were extended by it. This severity, which a man turns against himself, or against his fellow-creatures, and makes him either the victim or the oppressor, soon exerted itself against the Quakers. They were whipped, banished, and imprisoned. The proud simplicity of these new enthusiasts, who in the midst of tortures and ignominy praised God, and called for blessings upon men, inspired a reverence for their persons and opinions, and gained them a number of proselytes. This circumstance exasperated their persecutors, and hurried them on to the most atrocious acts of violence; and they caused five of them, who had returned clandestinely from banishment, to be hanged. It seemed as if the English had come to America to exercise upon their own countrymen the same cruelty the Spaniards had used against the Indians. This spirit of persecution

tion was at last suppressed by the interposition of the mother country, from whence it had been brought.

Cromwell was no more: enthusiasm, hypocrisy, and fanaticism, which composed his character; factions, rebellions, and proscriptions; were all buried with him, and England had the prospect of calmer days. Charles the second, at his restoration, had introduced amongst his subjects a social turn, a taste for convivial pleasures, gallantry, and diversions; and for all those amusements he had been engaged in while he was wandering from one court to another in Europe, to recover the crown which his father had lost upon a scaffold. Nothing but such a total change of manners could possibly have secured the tranquillity of his government upon a throne marked with blood. He was one of those voluptuaries, whom the love of sensual pleasures sometimes excites to sentiments of compassion and humanity. Moved with the sufferings of the Quakers, he put a stop to them by a proclamation in 1661; but he was never able totally to extinguish the spirit of persecution that prevailed in America.

The colony had placed at their head Henry Vane, the son of that Sir Henry Vane, who had had such a remarkable share in the disturbances of his country. This obstinate and enthusiastic young man, in every thing
re-

resembling his father, unable either to live peaceably himself, or to suffer others to remain quiet, had contrived to revive the obscure and obsolete questions of grace and free will. The disputes upon these points ran very high; and would, probably, have plunged the colony into a civil war, if several of the savage nations united had not happened at that very time to fall upon the plantations of the disputants, and to massacre great numbers of them. The colonists, heated with their theological contests, paid at first very little attention to this considerable loss. But the danger at length became so urgent and so general, that all took up arms. As soon as the enemy was repulsed, the colony resumed its former dissentions; and the frenzy which they excited, broke out, in 1692, in a war, marked with as many atrocious instances of violence as any ever recorded in history.

There lived in a town of New England, called Salem, two young women who were subject to convulsions, accompanied with extraordinary symptoms. Their father, minister of the church, thought that they were bewitched; and having in consequence cast his suspicions upon an Indian girl who lived in his house, he compelled her by harsh treatment to confess that she was a witch. Other women, upon hearing this, seduced by the pleasure of exciting the public attention, immediately believed that the convulsions which proceeded only from the nature of their sex, were owing to the same cause. Three citizens, pitched upon by chance, were immediately thrown into prison, accused of witchcraft, hanged, and their bodies left exposed to wild beasts and birds of prey. A few days after, sixteen other persons, together with a counsellor, who, because he refused to plead against them, was supposed to share in their guilt, suffered in the same manner. From this instant, the imagination of the multitude was inflamed with these horrid and gloomy scenes. The innocence of youth, the infirmities of age, virgin modesty, fortune, honour, virtue, the most dignified employments of the state, nothing was sufficient to exempt from the suspicions of a people infatuated with visionary superstition. Children of ten years of age were put to death; young girls were stripped naked, and the marks of witchcraft searched for upon their bodies with the most indecent curiosity; those spots of the scurvy which age impresses upon the bodies of old men, were taken for evident signs of the infernal power. Fanaticism, wickedness, and vengeance, united, selected out their victims with pleasure. In default of witnesses, torments were employed to extort confessions dictated by the executioners

cutioners themselves. If the magistrates, tired out with executions, refused to punish, they were themselves accused of the crimes they would no longer pursue; the very ministers of religion raised false witnesses against them, who made them forfeit with their lives the tardy remorse excited in them by humanity. Dreams, apparitions, terror and consternation of every kind, increased these prodigies of folly and horror. The prisons were filled, the gibbets left standing, and all the citizens involved in gloomy apprehensions. The most prudent persons quitted a country imbrued with the blood of its inhabitants; and those that remained sought for nothing but rest in the grave. In a word, nothing less than the total and immediate subversion of the colony was expected; when on a sudden, in the height of the storm, the waves subsided, and a calm ensued. All eyes were opened at once, and the excess of the evil awakened the minds which it had at first stupified. Bitter and painful remorse was the immediate consequence; the mercy of God was implored by a general fast, and public prayers were offered up to ask forgiveness for the presumption of having supposed that heaven could have been pleased with sacrifices with which it could only have been offended.

Posterity will probably never know exactly

actly what was the cause or remedy of this dreadful disorder. It had, perhaps, its first origin in the melancholy which these persecuted enthusiasts had brought with them from their own country, which had increased with the scurvy they had contracted at sea, and which had gathered fresh strength from the vapours and exhalations of a soil newly broken up, as well as from the inconveniences and hardships inseparable from a change of climate and manner of living. The contagion, however, ceased like all other epidemical distempers, exhausted by its very communication; as all the disorders of the imagination are dispelled in the transports of a delirium. A perfect calm succeeded this agitation; and the puritans of New-England have never since been seized with so gloomy a fit of enthusiasm.

3. *Government, Population, Cultures, Manufactures, Trade, and Navigation, of New England.*

THIS colony, bounded to the north by Canada, to the west by New-York, and to the east and south by Nova Scotia and the ocean, extends full three hundred miles on the borders of the sea, and upwards of fifty miles in the inland parts.

The clearing of the lands is not done by chance

chance as in the other provinces. From the firſt they were ſubjected to laws which are ſtill religiouſly obſerved. No citizen whatever has the liberty of ſettling even upon unoccupied land. The government, which was deſirous of preſerving all its members from the inroads of the ſavages, and that they ſhould be at hand to partake of the ſuccours of a well reguiated ſociety, hath ordered that whole villages ſhould be formed at once. As ſoon as ſixty families offer to build a church, maintain a clergyman, and pay a ſchoolmaſter, the general congreſs allot them a ſituation, and permit them to have two repreſentatives in the legiſlative body of the colony. The diſtrict aſſigned them always borders upon the lands already cleared, and generally contains ſix thouſand ſquare acres. Theſe new people chuſe out the ſpot moſt convenient for their reſpective habitations, and it is uſually of a ſquare figure. The church is placed in the centre; and the coloniſts dividing the land among themſelves, each incloſes his property with a hedge. Some woods are reſerved for a common. It is thus that New-England is continually aggrandizing itſelf, without diſcontinuing to make one complete and well-conſtituted province.

Though the colony is ſituated in the midſt of the temperate zone, yet the climate is not
ſo

so mild as that of some European provinces which are under the same parallel. The winters are longer, and more cold; the summers shorter, and more hot. The sky is commonly clear, and the rains more plentiful than lasting. The air has grown purer since its circulation has been made free by cutting down the woods; and malignant vapours, which at first carried off some of the inhabitants, are no longer complained of.

The country is divided into four provinces, which in the beginning had no connection with one another. The necessity of maintaining an armed force against the savages obliged them to form a confederacy in 1643, at which time they took the name of the United Colonies. In consequence of this league, two deputies from each establishment used to meet in a stated place to deliberate upon the common affairs of New-England, according to the instructions they had received from the assembly by which they were sent. This association controuled in no one point the right which every individual had of acting entirely as he pleased, without either the permission or approbation of the mother country. All the submission of these provinces consisted in a vague acknowledgment of the kings of Britain for their sovereigns.

So slight a dependence displeased Charles II.
The

The province of Massachuset's bay, which, though the smallest, was the richest and the most populous of the four, being guilty of some misdemeanour against government, the king seized that opportunity of taking away its charter in 1684; and it remained without one till the revolution; when it received another, which, however, did not answer its claims or expectations. The crown reserved to itself the right of nominating the governor, and appointing to all military employments and to all principal posts in the civil and juridical departments: allowing the people of the colony their legislative power, they gave the governor a negative voice and the command of the troops, which secured him a sufficient influence to enable him to maintain the prerogative of the mother country in all its force. The provinces of Connecticut and Rhode-Island, by timely submission, prevented the punishment that of Massachuset had incurred, and retained their original charter. That of New-Hampshire had been always regulated by the same mode of administration as the province of Massachuset's bay. The same governor presides over the whole colony, but with regulations adapted to the constitution of each province. According to the most exact calculations, the present population of New-England is computed at four hundred thousand inhabitants, which

are

are more numerous to the south than to the north of the colony, where the soil is less fertile. Among such a number of citizens, there are few proprietors wealthy enough to leave the care of their plantations to stewards or farmers: most of them are planters in easy circumstances, who live upon their estates and are busied in the labours of the field. This equality of fortune, joined to the religious principles and to the nature of the government, gives this people a more republican cast than is to be observed in the other colonies.

None of our best fruits have degenerated New-England; it is even said, that the apple is improved, at least it has multiplied exceedingly, and made cyder a more common drink than in any other part of the world. All our roots and garden-stuff have had the same success; but the seeds have not thriven quite so well. Wheat is apt to be blighted, barley grows dry, and oats yield more straw than grain. In default of these the maize, which is usually consumed in making beer, is the resource of the common people. There are large and fruitful meadows, which are covered with numerous flocks.

The arts, though carried to a greater degree of perfection in this colony than in any of the others, have not made near the same progress as agriculture. There are not more than

than four or five manufactures of any importance.

The first which was formed, was that for building of ships. It maintained for a long time a degree of reputation. The vessels out of this dock were in great estimation, the materials of which they were constructed being found much less porous and much less apt to split than those of the more southern provinces. Since 1730, the numbers of them are considerably diminished, because the woods for building have been little attended to, and used for other purposes. To prevent this inconvenience, it was proposed to forbid the cutting of any of them within ten miles of the sea; and we know not for what reason this law, the necessity of which was so evident, was never put in force. The distilling of rum has succeeded better than the building of ships. It was begun from the facility the New-Englanders had of importing large quantities of melasses from the Caribbees. The melasses were at first used in kind for various purposes. By degrees they learnt to distil them. When made into rum, they supplied the neighbouring savages with it, as the Newfoundland fishermen did the other northern provinces, and sailors who frequented the coast of Africa. The degree of imperfection in which this art hath still remained in the colony, has not diminished the sale of it;

it; becaufe they have always been able to afford the rum at a very low price.

The fame reafon has both fupported and increafed the manufacture of hats. Though limited by the regulations of the mother country to the internal confumption of the colony, the merchants have found means to furmount thefe obftacles, and to fmuggle pretty large quantities of them into the neighbouring fettlements.

The colony fells no cloths, but it buys very few. The fleeces of its flocks, as long, tho' not quite fo fine, as the Englifh ones, make coarfe ftuffs, which do extremely well for plain men who live in the country.

Some Prefbyterians who were driven from the north of Ireland by the perfecutions either of the government or of the clergy, firft taught the New Englanders to cultivate hemp and flax, and to manufacture them. The linens made of them are fince become one of the great refources of the colony.

The mother country, whofe political calculations have not always coincided with the high opinion entertained of her abilities, has omitted nothing to thwart thefe feveral manufactures. She did not perceive, that, by this oppreffive conduct of the government, thofe of her fubjects who were employed in clearing this confiderable part of the new world muft be reduced to the alternative either of aban-

abandoning fo good a country, or procuring from among themfelves the things of general ufe and of immediate neceffity. Indeed, even thefe refources would not have been fufficient to maintain them, if they had not had the good fortune and the addrefs to open to themfelves feveral other channels of fubfiftence, the origin and progrefs of which we muft endeavour to trace.

The firft refource they met with from without, was in the fifhery. It has been encouraged to fuch a degree, that a regulation has taken place, by which every family who fhould declare that it had lived upon falt-fifh for two days in the week during a whole year, fhould be difburdened of part of their tax. Thus commercial views enjoin abftinence from meat to the proteftants, in the fame manner as religion prefcribes it to the catholics.

Mackerel is caught only in the fpring at the mouth of the Pentagouet, a confiderable river which empties itfelf in Fundy bay, towards the extremity of the colony. In the very centre of the coaft, and near Bofton, the cod-fifh is always in fuch plenty, that Cape Cod, notwithftanding the fterility of its foil, is one of the moft populous parts of the country. Not content, however, with the fifh caught in its own latitudes, New England fends every year about two hundred veffels, from thirty-five to forty tons each, to the great bank, to Newfoundland, and to Cape Breton, which commonly make three voyages a feafon, and bring back at leaft a hundred thoufand quintals of cod. Befides, there are larger veffels which fail from the fame ports, and exchange provifions for the produce of the fifhery of thofe Englifh who are fettled in thefe frozen and barren regions. All this cod is afterwards diftributed in the fouthern parts of Europe and America.

This is not the only article with which the Britifh iflands in the new world are fupplied by New England. It furnifhes them, befides, horfes, oxen, hogs, falt meat, butter, tallow, cheefe, flour, bifcuit, Indian corn, peafe, fruits, cyder, hemp, flax, and woods of all kinds. The fame commodities pafs into the iflands belonging to the other nations, fometimes openly, fometimes by fmuggling, but always in leffer quanties during peace than in time of war. Honduras, Surinam, and other parts of the American continent open fimilar markets to New England. This province alfo fetches wines and brandies from the Madeiras and the Azores, and pays for them with cod-fifh and corn.

The ports of Italy, Spain, and Portugal, receive annually fixty or feventy of their fhips. They come there laden with cod, wood for fhip-building, naval ftores, corn, and fifh-oil;

oil; many of them return with olive-oil, falt, wine, and money, immediately to New England, where they land their cargoes clandeftinely. By this method, they elude the cuftoms they would be obliged to pay in Great Britain, if they went there, as in purfuance of a pofitive order they ought to do. The fhips which do not return to the original port are fold in thofe where they difpofe of their cargo. They have frequently no particular addrefs, but are freighted indifferently for every merchant and every port, till they meet with a proper purchafer.

The mother country receives from this colony yards and mafts for the royal navy, planks, pot-afhes, pitch, tar, turpentine, a few furs, and in years of fcarcity fome corn. Thefe cargoes come home in fhips built by her own merchants, or bought by them of privateers, who build upon fpeculation.

Befides the trade New England makes of her own productions, fhe has appropriated great part of the conveying trade between North and South America, in confequence of which the New Englanders are looked upon as the brokers or Hollanders of that part of the world.

Notwithftanding this lively and continued exertion, New England has never yet been able to free herfelf from debt. She has never been able to pay exactly for what fhe received

ved from the mother country, either in productions of her own or of foreign industry, or in those from the East-Indies; all which articles of trade amount annually to 393,750 *l.*

She has still, however, trade enough to keep six thousand sailors in constant employment. Her marine consists of five hundred large vessels, which carry all together forty thousand tons burden; besides a great number of smaller vessels for fishing and for the coasting trade, which come out indifferently from all the open roads which are spread all over the coast. Almost all of them load and unload at Boston.

BOSTON, the capital of New England, is situated in a peninsula, about four miles long, at the bottom of the fine bay of Massachuset, which reaches about eight miles within land. The opening of the bay is sheltered from the impetuosity of the waves by a number of rocks which rise above the water; and by a dozen of small islands, the greater part of which are fruitful and inhabited. These dykes and natural ramparts will not allow more than three ships to come in together. At the end of the last century, a regular citadel, named Fort William, was erected in one of the islands upon this narrow channel. There are one hundred pieces of cannon, carrying forty-two pounders each,

upon

upon it, which are difposed in such a manner, that they can batter a ship fore and aft before it is possible for her to bring her guns to bear. A league further on, there is a very high light-house, the signals from which, in case of invasion, are perceived and repeated by the fortresses along the whole coast; at the same time that Boston has her own lighthouses, which spread the alarm to all the inland country. Except in the case of a very thick fog, which a few ships may take advantage of to get into some of the smaller islands, the town has always five or six hours to prepare for the reception of the enemy, and to get together ten thousand militia, which can be raised at four and twenty hours notice. If a fleet should ever be able to pass the artillery of Fort William, it would infallibly be stopped by a couple of batteries, which being erected to the north and south of the place, command the whole bay, and would give time for all the vessels and commercial stores to be sheltered from cannon shot in the river Charles.

Boston port is large enough for six hundred vessels to anchor in it safely and commodiously. There is a magnificent pier constructed, far enough advanced in the sea for the ships to unload their goods without the assistance of a lighter, and to discharge them into the warehouses which are ranged on the north side. At the extremity of the pier the town appears, built in the form of a crescent round the harbour. According to the bills of mortality, which are become with reason the only rule of political arithmetic, it contains about thirty thousand inhabitants, composed of Anabaptists, Quakers, French refugees, English Presbyterians, and Church-of-England men. The houses, furniture, dress, food, conversation, customs, and manners, are so exactly similar to the mode of living in London, that it is impossible to find any other difference but that which arises from the overgrown population of large capitals.

CHAP. X.

Of NEW YORK and NEW JERSEY.

1. *New York, founded by the Dutch, passes into the hands of the English.*

NEW-YORK, limited to the east by New-England, and bounded to the west by New-Jersey, occupies at first a very narrow space of twenty miles along the sea-shore, and, insensibly enlarging, extends above a hundred and fifty miles northward in the inland country.

This country was discovered by Henry Hudson in 1609. That celebrated navigator,

after

after having made vain attempts under the patronage of the Dutch East-India company for the discovery of a north-west passage, veered about to the southward, and coasted along the continent, in hopes of making some useful discovery that might prove a kind of indemnification to the society for the trust they had reposed in him. He entered into a considerable river, to which he gave his name; and after having reconnoitred the coast and its inhabitants, returned to Amsterdam from whence he had set sail.

According to the European system, which considers the people of the new world as nothing, this country should have belonged to the Dutch. It had been discovered by a man in their service, who had taken possession of it in their name, and given up to them all the claims which he himself might have to it. His being an Englishman did not in the least invalidate these uncontrovertable titles. It must, therefore, have occasioned great surprise, when James I. asserted his pretensions to it, upon the principle that Hudson was born his subject; as if the real country of any man was not that in which he earns his subsistence. The king was so convinced of this, that he soon gave up the matter; and the republic sent in 1610 to lay the foundation of the colony in a country which was to be called **New Belgia**. Every thing prospered here.

here. Fortunate beginnings seemed to announce a still greater progress, when in 1664 the colony was exposed to a storm which it could not possibly foresee.

England, which had not at that time those intimate connections with Holland that the ambition and successes of Lewis XIV. have given birth to since, had long seen with a jealous eye the prosperity of a small state in its neighbourhood, which, though but just formed, was always extending its prosperous trade to all parts of the world. She was secretly disturbed at the thoughts of not being on an equality with a power to whom, in the nature of things, she ought to have been greatly superior. These rivals in commerce and navigation, by their vigilance and oeconomy, gained the advantage over her in all the large markets of the whole universe. Every effort she made to establish a competition turned either to her loss or discredit, and she was obliged only to act a secondary part, whilst all the trade then known was evidently centering itself in the republic. At length, the nation felt the disgrace of her merchants; and resolved, that what they could not compass by industry should be secured to them by force. Charles II. notwithstanding his aversion for business, and his immoderate love of pleasure, eagerly adopted a measure which gave him a prospect of acquiring the riches

riches of thefe diftant regions, together with the maritime empire of Europe. His brother, more active and more enterprifing than himfelf, encouraged him in thefe difpofitions; and the deliberation concluded with their ordering the Dutch fhips to be attacked, without any previous declaration of war.

An Englifh fleet appeared before New Belgia in the month of Auguft. It had three thoufand men on board; and fo numerous a force precluding every idea as well as every hope of refiftance, the colony fubmitted as foon as it was fummoned. The conqueft was fecured to the victors by the treaty of Breda; but it was again taken from them in 1673, when the intrigues of France had found means to fet two powers at variance, who for their mutual interefts ought always to be friends. A fecond treaty reftored New Belgia to the Englifh, who have remained in quiet poffeffion of it ever fince under the name of New York.

It had taken that name from the duke of York, to whom it had been given by the king in 1664. As foon as he had recovered it, he governed it upon the fame arbitrary principles which afterwards deprived him of the throne. His deputies, in whofe hands were lodged powers of every kind, not contented with the exercife of the public authority, conftituted themfelves arbitrators in all
pri-

private disputes. The country was then inhabited by Hollanders who had preferred these plantations to their own country, and by colonists who had come from New England. These people had been too long accustomed to liberty, to submit patiently for any time to so arbitrary an administration. Every thing seemed tending either to an insurrection or an emigration, when in 1683 the colony was invited to chuse representatives to settle its form of government. Time produced some other changes; but it was not till 1691 that a fixed plan of government was adopted, which has been followed ever since.

At the head of the colony is a governor appointed by the crown; which likewise appoints twelve counsellors, without whose concurrence the governor can sign no act. The commons are represented by twenty-seven deputies, chosen by the inhabitants; and these several bodies constitute the general assembly, in which every power is lodged. The duration of this assembly, originally unlimited, was afterwards fixed at three years, and now continues for seven, like the British parliament, whose revolutions it has followed.

2. *Flou-*

2. *Flourishing state of New York. Causes of its prosperity.*

SUPPORTED upon a government so solid, so favourable to that liberty which makes every thing prosper, the colony gave itself up entirely to all the labours which its situation could require or encourage. A climate much milder than that of New England, a soil superior to it for the cultivation of corn, and equally fit for that of every other production, soon enabled it to vie succesfsully with an establishment that had got the start of it in all its productions and in all the markets. If it was not equal in its manufactures, this inferiority was amply compensated by a fur-trade infinitely more considerable. These means of prosperity, united to a very great degree of toleration in religious matters, have raised its population to one hundred and fifty thousand inhabitants; five and twenty thousand of whom are able to bear arms, and constitute the national militia.

The colony would still have flourished much more, had not its prosperity been obstructed by the fanaticism of two governors, the oppressive conduct of some others, and the extravagant grants made to some individuals in too high favour; but these inconveniences, which are only temporary under the
British

British government, have some of them ceased, and the rest of them are lessened. The province may, therefore, expect to see her productions doubly increased, if the two thirds of its territory, which still remain uncleared, should yield as much as the one third which has already been cultivated.

It is impossible to foresee what influence these riches may have upon the minds of the inhabitants; but it is certain they have not yet abused those they have hitherto acquired. The Dutch, who were the first founders of the colony, planted in it that spirit of order and oeconomy which is the characteristic of of their nation; and as they always made up the bulk of the people, even after these had changed masters, the example of their decent manners was imitated by all the new colonists brought amongst them by the conquest. The Germans, compelled to take refuge in America by the persecution which drove them out of the Palatinate or from the other provinces of the empire, were naturally inclined to this simple and modest way of life; and the English and French, who were not accustomed to so much frugality, soon conformed, either from motives of wisdom or emulation, to a mode of living less expensive and more familiar than that which is regulated by fashion and parade.

What has been the consequence? That the colony

colony has never run in debt with the mother country; that it has by that means preserved an entire liberty in its sales and purchases, and been enabled always to give to its affairs the direction which has been most advantageous to them. Had the representatives carried the same principles into their administration, the province would not have entered precipitately into engagements, the burden of which it already feels.

Both the banks of Hudson's river are laid out in the plantations of the colony, which enliven and decorate these borders. It is upon this magnificent canal, which is navigable day and night, in all seasons, and where the tide runs up above a hundred and sixty miles in the land, that every thing which is intended for the general market is embarked in vessels of forty or fifty tons burden. The staple itself, which is near the sea, is extremely well situated for receiving all the merchandise of the province, and all that comes from LONG ISLAND, which is only separated from the continent by a narrow channel.

This island, which takes its name from its figure, is one hundred and twenty miles in length by twelve in breadth. It was formerly very famous for the great number of whales and sea-calves taken in its neighbourhood; but whether it is that the frequent fisheries have driven away these animals, which generally

rally seek quiet seas and desert shores, they have disappeared, and another branch of industry has been found to supply their loss. As the pastures are most excellent, the breeding of all kinds of cattle, and particularly horses, has been much attended to, without neglecting any other branch of cultivation. All these different riches flow to the principal market, which is also increased by productions brought from a greater distance. Some parts of New England and New Jersey find their account in pouring their stores into this magazine.

This mart is a very considerable town, which at present has the same name as the colony, and is called NEW YORK. It was formerly built by the Dutch, who gave it the name of New Amsterdam, in an island called Manahatton, which is fourteen leagues long and not very broad. In 1756, its population amounted to 10,468 whites, and 2,275 negroes. There is not any town where the air is better, or where there is a more general appearance of ease and plenty. Both the public edifices and private houses convey the idea of solidity united to convenience. If the city, however, were attacked with vigour, it would hardly hold out twenty-four hours, having no other defence of the road or the town except a bad fort and a stone retrenchment.

New York, which stands at the distance of about two miles from the mouth of Hudson's river, has, properly speaking, neither port or bason; but it does not want either, because its road is sufficient. It is from thence that 250 or 300 ships are dispatched every year for the different ports of Europe and America. England receives but a small part of them; but they are the richest, because they are those whose cargo consists in furs and beaver skins. The manner in which the colony gets possession of these peltries is now to be explained.

As soon as the Dutch had built New Amsterdam in a situation which they thought favourable for the intercourse with Europe, they next endeavoured to establish an advantageous trade there. The only thing at that time in request from North America was furs; but as the neighbouring savages offered but few, and those indifferent ones, there was a necessity of pushing to the north to have them better and in larger quantities. In consequence of this, a project was formed for an establishment on the banks of Hudson's river, 150 miles distance from the capital. The circumstances fortunately proved favourable for obtaining the consent of the Iroquois, to whom the territory required belonged. This brave nation happened to be then at war with the French, who were just arrived in Canada.

Upon

Upon an agreement to supply them with the same arms that their enemies used, they allowed the Dutch to build Fort Orange, which was afterwards called Fort Albany. There was never the least dispute between the two nations; on the contrary, the Dutch, with the assistance of their powder, lead, and guns, which they used to give in exchange for skins, secured to themselves not only what they could get by their own hunting in all the five countries, but even the spoils collected by the Iroquois warriors in their expeditions.

Though the English, upon their taking possession of the colony, maintained the union with the savages, they did not think seriously of extending the fur-trade, till the revocation of the edict of Nantes in 1685 introduced among them the art of making beaver hats. Their efforts were for a long time ineffectual, and there were chiefly two obstacles to their success. The French were accustomed to draw from Albany itself coverlets, thick worsted stuffs, different iron and copper manufactures, even arms and ammunition; all which they could sell to the savages with so much the more advantage as these goods bought at Albany cost them one third less than they would have done any other way. Besides, the American nations, who were separated from New York by the country of the Iroquois, in which nobody chose to venture far, could hardly treat with any but the French.

Burnet, who was governor of the British colony in 1720, was either the first who saw the evil, or the first who ventured to strike at the root of it. He made the general assembly forbid all communication between Albany and Canada, and then obtained the consent of the Iroquois to build and fortify the factory of Oswego at his own expence, on that part of the lake Ontario by which most of the savages must pass in their way to Montreal. In consequence of these two operations, the beavers and the other peltries were pretty equally divided between the French and British. The accession of Canada cannot but increase at present the share New York had in the trade, as the latter is better situated for it than the country which disputed it with her.

If the British colony has gained by the acquisition of Canada, it does not appear to have lost any thing by being separated from New Jersey, which formerly made a part of New Belgia, under the title of New Sweden.

3. *In what manner New Jersey fell into the hands of the English. Its present state.*

THE Swedes were, in fact, the first Europeans

peans who settled in this region about the year 1639. The neglect in which they were left by their own country, which was too weak to be able to extend its protection to them at so great a distance, obliged them, at the end of sixteen years, to give themselves up to the Dutch, who united this acquisition to New Belgia. When the duke of York received the grant of the two countries, he separated them; and divided the least of them, called New Jersey, between two of his favourites.

Carteret and Berkley, the first of whom had received the eastern, and the other the western part of the province, had solicited this vast territory with no other view but to put it up to sale. Several adventurers accordingly bought large districts of them at a low price, which they divided and sold again in smaller parcels. In the midst of these subdivisions, the colony became divided into two distinct provinces, each separately governed by the original proprietors. The exercise of this right growing at length inconvenient, as indeed it was ill adapted to the situation of a subject, they gave up their charter to the crown in 1702; and from that time the two provinces became one, and were directed, like the greater part of the other British colonies, by a governor, a council, and a general assembly.

New

New Jerfey, fituated between 39 and 40 degrees north latitude, is bounded to the eaſt by New York, to the weſt by Penfylvania, to the north by unknown land, and to the fouth by the ocean, which waſhes its coaſts thro' an extent of 120 miles. This large country before the laſt revolution contained only fixteen thoufand inhabitants, the defcendants of Swedes and Dutch, who were its firſt cultivators, to whom had been added fome Quakers, and fome Church-of-England men, with a greater number of Preſbyterians. The defect of the government ſtopped the progreſs and occafioned the indigence of this fmall colony. It might, therefore, have been expected that the æra of liberty ſhould have been that of its profperity; but almoſt all the Europeans who went to the new world in fearch either of an afylum or riches, preferring the milder and more fruitful climates of Carolina and Penfylvania; New Jerfey could never recover from its primitive languor. Even at this day, it does not reckon above fifty thoufand whites, united in villages, or difperfed among the plantations, with twenty thoufand blacks.

The poverty of this province not fuffering it in the beginning to open a direct trade with the diſtant or foreign markets, it began to fell its productions at Philadelphia, and efpecially at New York, with which there was an easy communication by rivers. It has continued this practice ever since, and receives in exchange from the two cities some of the productions of the mother country. Far, however, from being able to acquire any objects of luxury, it cannot even afford to purchase all the articles of immediate necessity; but is obliged itself to manufacture the greatest part of its clothing.

There is of course very little specie in the colony, which is reduced to the use of paper-currency. All its bills together do not amount to more than 59,062*l.* 10*s.* As they are current both in Pensylvania and New York, which do not take any of each others bills; they bear an advanced premium above the bills of these two colonies, by being made use of in all the payments between them.

But so trifling an advantage will never give any real importance to New Jersey. It is from out of its own bosom, that is, from the culture of its immense tract of desert country, that it is to draw its vigour and prosperity. As long as it stands in need of intermediate agents, it will never recover from the state of languor into which it is plunged. This the colony is thoroughly sensible of; and all its efforts are now directed to this end, in order to enable it to act for itself. It has even already made some with success. As far back as the year 1751, it found means to fit

fit out, at its own expence, thirty-eight veffels, bound to Europe or to the fouthern ifles
of America. Thefe veffels carried 188,000
quintals of bifcuits, fix thoufand four hundred and twenty-four barrels of flour, feven-
teen thoufand nine hundred and forty-one
bufhels of corn, three hundred and fourteen
barrels of falt beef and pork, fourteen hundred quintals of hemp; together with a pretty
large quantity of hams, butter, beer, linfeed,
iron in bars, and wood for building. It is
imagined that this direct trade may have increafed one third fince that time.

This beginning of riches muft raife the
emulation, the induftry, the hopes, the projects, and the interprifes of a colony, which
hitherto had not been able to fuftain the part
in trade which its fituation feemed to promife it. If, however, there are fome poor
and feeble ftates that draw their fubfiftence
and fupport from the vicinity of others more
rich and more brilliant than themfelves,
there are a far greater number whom fuch a
neighbourhood entirely crufhes and deftroys.
Such, perhaps, has been the fate of New
Jerfey, as will appear from the hiftory we
are going to give of Penfylvania; which, lying too clofe to this colony, has fometimes
ftifled it with its fhadow, fometimes eclipfed
it with its fplendor.

BOOK II.

BRITISH COLONIES FOUNDED IN PENSYLVANIA, VIRGINIA, MARYLAND, CAROLINA, GEORGIA, AND FLORIDA.

CHAP. I.
Of Pensylvania.

1. *The Quakers found Penſylvania. Manners of that ſect.*

LUTHERANISM, which was deſtined to cauſe a remarkable change in Europe, either by its own influence, or by the example it gave, had occaſioned a great fermentation in the minds of all men; when there aroſe from the midſt of it a new religion, which at firſt appeared much more like a rebellion guided by fanaticiſm, than like a ſect that was governed by any fixed principles. In fact, the generality of innovators follow a regular ſyſtem, compoſed of doctrines connected with each other; and, in the
be-

beginning at least, take arms only to defend themselves. The Anabaptists, on the contrary, as if they had looked into the Bible only for the word of command to attack, lifted up the standard of rebellion, before they had agreed upon a system of doctrine. It is true, indeed, that their leaders had taught, that it was a ridiculous and useless practice to administer baptism to infants; and asserted that their opinion upon this point was the same as that of the primitive church: but they had not yet ever practised themselves this only article of faith, which furnished a pretence for separation. The spirit of sedition precluded them from paying a proper attention to the schismatic tenets on which their division was founded. To shake off the tyrannical yoke of church and state, was their law and their faith. To enlist in the armies of the Lord; to join with the faithful, who were to wield the sword of Gideon; this was their device, their motive, and their signal for rallying.

It was not till after they had carried fire and sword into a great part of Germany, that the Anabaptists thought at last of marking and cementing their confederacy by some visible sign of union. Having been inspired at first to raise a body of troops, in 1525 they were inspired to compose a religious code, and the following were the tenets they adopted.

In the mixed fyftem of intolerance and mildnefs by which they are guided, the Anabaptift church, being the only one in which the pure word of God is taught, neither can nor ought to communicate with any other.

The fpirit of the Lord blowing wherefoever it lifteth, the power of preaching is not limited to one order of the faithful, but is given to all. Every one likewife has the gift of prophecy.

Every fect which has not preferved the community of all things, which conftituted the life and fpirit of Chriftianity, has degenerated, and is for that reafon an impure fociety.

Magiftrates are ufelefs in a fociety of the truly faithful. A Chriftian never has occafion for any; nor is a Chriftian allowed to be one himfelf.

Chriftians are not permitted to take up arms even in their own defence, much lefs is it lawful for them to inlift as foldiers in mercenary armies.

Both law-fuits and oaths are forbidden the difciples of Chrift; who has commanded them to let their yea be yea, and their nay nay.

The baptifm of infants is an invention of the devil and of the pope. The validity of baptifm depends upon the voluntary confent of the adults, who alone are able to receive

it

it with a confcioufnefs of the engagement they take upon themfelves.

Such was, in its origin, the religious fyftem of the Anabaptifts. Tho' it appears founded on charity and mildnefs, yet it produced nothing but violence and iniquity. The chimerical idea of an equality of ftations is the moft dangerous one that can be adopted in a civilized fociety. To preach this fyftem to the people, is not to put them in mind of their rights, it is leading them on to affaffination and plunder. It is letting domeftic animals loofe, and transforming them into wild beafts. The mafters who govern the people muft be better informed, or the laws by which they are conducted muft be foftened: but there is in fact no fuch thing in nature as a real equality; it exifts only in the fyftem of equity. Even the favages themfelves are not equal, when once they are collected into hords. They are only fo, while they wander in the woods; and then the man who fuffers the produce of his chafe to be taken from him, is not the equal of him who deprives him of it. Such has been the origin of all focieties.

A doctrine, the bafis of which was the community of goods and equality of ranks, was hardly calculated to find partizans any where but among the poor. The peafants, accordingly, all adopted it with the more
vio-

violence in proportion as the yoke from which it delivered them was more infupportable. The far greater part, efpecially thofe who were condemned to flavery, rofe up in arms on all fides, to fupport a doctrine, which, from being vaffals, made them equal to their lords. The apprehenfion of feeing one of the firft bands of fociety, obedience to the magiftrate, broken, united all other fects againft them, who could not fubfift without fubordination. After having carried on a more obftinate refiftance than could have been expected, they yielded at length to the number of their enemies. Their fect, notwithftanding it had made its way all over Germany, and into a part of the north, was no where prevalent, becaufe it had been every where oppofed and difperfed. It was but juft tolerated in thofe countries in which the greateft latitude of opinion was allowed; and there was not any ftate in which it was able to fettle a church, authorifed by the civil power. This of courfe weakened it, and from obfcurity it fell into contempt. Its only glory is that of having, perhaps, contributed to the foundation of the fect of the Quakers.

This humane and pacific fect had arifen in England amidft the confufions of a war, which terminated in a monarch's being dragged to the fcaffold by his own fubjects. The founder of it, George Fox, was of the lower clafs class of the people; a man who had been formerly a mechanic, but whom a singular and contemplative turn of mind had induced to quit his profession. In order to wean himself entirely from all earthly affections, he broke off all connections with his own family; and for fear of being tempted to renew them, he determined to have no fixed abode. He often wandered alone in the woods, without any other amusement but his bible. In time he even learnt to go without that, when he thought he had acquired from it a degree of inspiration similar to that of the apostles and the prophets.

Then he began to think of making proselytes, which he found not in the least difficult in a country where the minds of all men were filled and disturbed with enthusiastic notions. He was, therefore, soon followed by a multitude of disciples, the novelty and singularity of whose notions upon incomprehensible subjects could not fail of attracting and fascinating all those who were fond of the marvellous.

The first thing by which they caught the eye was the simplicity of their dress; in which there was neither gold nor silver lace, nor embroidery, nor laces, nor ruffles, and from which they affected to banish every thing that was superfluous or unnecessary. They would not suffer either a button in the hat, or a plait
in

in the coat, becaufe it was poffible to do without them. Such an extraordinary contempt for eftablifhed modes reminded thofe who adopted it, that it became them to be more virtuous than the reft of men from whom they diftinguifhed themfelves by this external modefty.

All the external deferences which the pride and tyranny of mankind exact from thofe who are unable to refufe them, were difdained by the quakers, who difclaimed the names of Mafter and Servant. They condemned all titles as pride in thofe who claimed them, and as meannefs in thofe who beftowed them. They did not allow to any perfon whatever the appellation of Eminence or Excellence, and fo far they might be in the right; but they refufed to comply with thofe reciprocal marks of attention which we call politenefs, and in this they were to blame. The name of Friend, they faid, was not to be refufed by one Chriftian or citizen to another; but the ceremony of bowing they confidered as ridiculous and troublefome. To pull off one's hat they held to be a want of refpect to one's felf, in order to fhew it to others. They carried it fo far, that even the magiftrates could not draw from them any external token of reverence; but they addreffed both them and princes, according to the ancient majefty of

lan-

language, in the second person and in the singular number.

The austerity of their morals ennobled the singularity of their manners. The use of arms, considered in every light, appeared a crime to them. If it was to attack, it was violating the laws of humanity; if to defend one's self, it was breaking through those of Christianity. Universal peace was the gospel they had agreed to profess. If any one smote a quaker upon one cheek, he immediately presented the other; if any one asked for his coat, he offered his waistcoat too. Nothing could engage these equitable men to demand more than the lawful price for their work, or to take less than what they demanded. An oath, even before a magistrate and in a just cause, they deemed to be a profanation of the name of God, in any of the wretched disputes that arise between weak and perishable beings.

The contempt they had for the outward forms of politeness in civil life was changed into aversion for the ritual and ceremonial parts of religion. They looked upon churches merely as the parade of religion; they considered the sabbath as a pernicious idleness, and baptism and the Lord's supper as ridiculous symbols. For this reason they rejected all regular orders of clergy. Every one of the faithful they imagined received an immediate illumination from the Holy Ghost, which gave a character far superior to that of the priesthood. When they were assembled together, the first person who found himself inspired arose and imparted the lights he had received from heaven. Even women were often favoured with this gift of speech, which they called the gift of prophecy: sometimes many of these holy brethren spoke at the same time; but much more frequently a profound silence prevailed in their assemblies.

The enthusiasm occasioned both by their meditations and discourses, excited such a degree of sensibility in the nervous system, that it threw them into convulsions, for which reason they were called Quakers. To have cured these people in process of time of their folly, nothing more was requisite than to turn it into ridicule; but, instead of this, persecution contributed to make it more general. Whilst every other new sect met with encouragement, this was exposed to every kind of punishment; imprisonments, whippings, pillories, mad-houses, nothing was thought too terrible for bigots, whose only crime was that of wanting to be virtuous and reasonable over much. The constancy with which they bore their sufferings, at first excited compassion and afterwards admiration for them. Even Cromwel, who had been one of their most violent enemies,

because

because they used to insinuate themselves into his camps, and discourage his soldiers from their profession, gave them public marks of his esteem. His policy exerted itself in endeavouring to draw them into his party, in order to conciliate to himself a higher degree of respect and consideration: but they either eluded his invitations, or rejected them; and he afterwards confessed, that this was the only religion in which his guineas had taken no effect.

Amongst the several persons who cast a temporary lustre on the sect, the only one who deserves to be remembered by posterity is William Penn. He was the son of an admiral, who had been fortunate enough to be equally distinguished by Cromwel and the two Stuarts who held the reigns of government after him. This able seaman, more supple and more insinuating than men commonly are in his profession, had made considerable advances to government in the different expeditions in which he had been engaged. The misfortunes of the times had not suffered them to be repaid during his life; and as affairs were not in a better situation at his death, it was proposed to his son, that, instead of money, he should accept of an immense territory in America. It was a country which, though long since discovered, and surrounded by English colonies, had always

ways been neglected. The love of humanity made him accept with pleasure this kind of patrimony, which was ceded to him almost as a sovereignty; and he determined to make it the abode of virtue, and the asylum of the unfortunate. With this generous design, towards the end of the year 1681, he set sail for his new possessions, which from that time took the name of Pensylvania. All the quakers were desirous to follow him, in order to avoid the persecution raised against them by the clergy on account of their not complying with the tithes and other ecclesiastical fees; but his prudence engaged him to take over no more than two thousand.

2. *Upon what principles Pensylvania was founded.*

Penn's arrival in the new world was signalized by an act of equity which made his person and principles equally beloved. Not thoroughly satisfied with the right given him to this extensive territory by the cession of the English ministry, he determined to make it his own property by purchasing it of the natives. The price he gave to the savages is not known; but though some people accuse them of stupidity for consenting to part with what they never ought to have alienated upon any terms; yet Penn is not the less entitled

titled to the glory of having given an example of moderation and justice in America, never so much as thought of before by the Europeans. He made his acquisition as valid as he could, and by the use he made of it he supplied any deficiency there might be in the legality of his title. The Americans conceived as great an affection for this colony as they had conceived an aversion for all those which had been founded in their neighbourhood without their consent. From that time there arose a mutual confidence between the two people, founded upon good faith, which nothing has ever been able to shake.

Penn's humanity could not be confined to the savages only; it extended itself to all those who were desirous of living under his laws. Sensible that the happiness of the people depended upon the nature of the legislation, he founded his upon those two first principles of public splendor and private felicity; liberty, and property. Here it is that the mind rests with pleasure upon modern history, and feels some kind of compensation for the disgust, horror, or melancholy, which the whole of it, but particularly the account of the European settlements in America, inspires. Hitherto we have only seen these barbarians spreading depopulation before they took possession, and laying every thing waſte before they cultivated. It is time to obſerve the ſeeds of reaſon, happineſs, and humanity, ſown and ſpringing up amidſt the ruin of an hemiſphere, which ſtill reeks with the blood of all its people, civilized as well as ſavage.

This virtuous legiſlator made toleration the baſis of his ſociety. He admitted every one who acknowledged a God to the rights of a citizen, and made every Chriſtian eligible to ſtate-employments. But he left every one at liberty to invoke the Supreme Being as he thought proper; and neither eſtabliſhed a reigning church in Penſylvania, nor exacted contributions for building places of public worſhip, nor compelled any perſons to attend them.

Jealous of immortalizing his name, he veſted in his family the right of nominating the chief governor of the colony: but he ordained that no profits ſhould be annexed to his employment, except ſuch as were voluntarily granted; and that he ſhould have no authority without the concurrence of the deputies of the people. All the citizens, who had an intereſt in the law, by having one in the circumſtance the law was intended to regulate, were to be electors and might be choſen. To avoid as much as poſſible every kind of corruption, it was ordained that the repreſentatives ſhould be choſen by ſuffrages

frages privately given. To establish a law, a plurality of voices was sufficient; but a majority of two thirds was necessary to settle a tax. Such a tax as this was certainly more like a free gift than a subsidy demanded by government; but was it possible to grant less indulgences to men who were come so far in search of peace?

Such was the opinion of that real philosopher Penn. He gave a thousand acres to all those who could afford to pay twenty pounds for them. Every one who could not, obtained for himself, his wife, each of his children above sixteen years, and each of his servants, fifty acres of land, for the annual quit-rent of about one penny per acre.

To fix these properties for ever, he established tribunals to protect the laws made for the preservation of property. But it is not protecting the property of lands to make those who are in possession of them purchase the law that secures them: for, in that case, one is obliged to give away part of one's property in order to secure the rest; and law, in process of time, exhausts the very treasures it should preserve, and the very property it should defend. Lest any persons should be found whose interest it might be to encourage or prolong law-suits, he forbade, under very strict penalties, all those who were engaged in the administration of justice, to receive any salary or gratification whatsoever. And further, every district was obliged to chuse three arbitrators, whose business it was to endeavour to prevent, and make up, any disputes that might happen, before they were carried into a court of justice.

This attention to prevent law-suits sprang from the desire of preventing crimes. All the laws, that they might have no vices to punish, were directed to put a stop to them even in their very sources, poverty and idleness. It was enacted, that every child above twelve years old should be obliged to learn a profession, let his condition be what it would. This regulation, at the same time that it secured the poor man a subsistence, furnished the rich man with a resource against every reverse of fortune; and preserved the natural equality of mankind, by recalling to every man's remembrance his original destination, which is that of labour either of the mind or of the body.

Such primary institutions would be necessarily productive of an excellent legislation; and accordingly the advantages of that established by Penn manifested itself in the rapid and continued prosperity of Pensylvania, which, without either wars, or conquests, or struggles, or any of those revolutions which attract the eyes of the vulgar,

gar, soon became an object fit to excite the admiration of the whole universe. Its neighbours, notwithstanding their savage state, were softened by the sweetness of its manners; and distant nations, notwithstanding their corruption, paid homage to its virtues. All were delighted to see those heroic days of antiquity realized, which European manners and laws had long taught every one to consider as entirely fabulous.

3. *Extent, climate, and soil, of Pensylvania. Its prosperity.*

PENSYLVANIA is defended to the east by the ocean, to the north by New York and New Jersey, to the south by Virginia and Maryland, to the west by the Indians; on all sides by friends, and within itself by the virtue of its inhabitants. Its coasts, which are flat rst very narrow, extend gradually to 120 miles; and the breadth of it, which has no other limits than its population and culture, already comprehends 145 miles. The sky of the colony is pure and serene; the climate, very wholesome of itself, has been rendered still more so by cultivation; the waters, equally salubrious and clear, always flow upon a bed of rock or sand; the year is tempered by the regular return of the seasons. Winter, which begins in the month of January,

nuary, lasts till the end of March. As it is seldom accompanied with clouds or fogs, the cold is, generally speaking, moderate; sometimes, however, sharp enough to freeze the largest rivers in one night. This revolution, which is as short as it is sudden, is occasioned by the north-west winds, which blow from the mountains and lakes of Canada. The spring is ushered in by soft rains, and by a gentle heat which increases gradually till the end of June. The heats of the dog-days would be insupportable, were it not for the refreshing breezes of the south-west wind; but this succour, though pretty constant, sometimes exposes them to hurricanes that blow down whole forests and tear up trees by the roots, especially in the neighbourhood of the sea, where they are most violent. The three autumnal months are commonly attended with no other inconvenience but that of being too rainy.

Though the country is unequal, it is not less fertile. The soil in some places consists of a yellow black sand, in others it is gravelly, and sometimes it is a greyish ash upon a stony bottom; generally speaking, it is a rich earth, particularly between the rivulets, which, intersecting it in all directions, contribute more to the fertility of the country than navigable rivers would.

When the Europeans first came into the country,

country, they found nothing in it but wood for building, and iron mines. In process of time, by cutting down the trees, and clearing the ground, they covered it with innumerable herds, with a great variety of fruits, with plantations of flax and hemp, with many kinds of vegetables, with every sort of grain, and especially with rye and maize; which a happy experience had shewn to be particularly proper to the climate. Cultivation was carried on in all parts with such vigour and success as excited the astonishment of all nations.

From whence could arise this extraordinary prosperity? From that civil and religious liberty which has attracted the Swedes, Dutch, French, and particularly some laborious Germans, into that country. It has been the joint work of Quakers, Anabaptists, Church-of-England men, Methodists, Presbyterians, Moravians, Lutherans, and Catholics.

Among the numerous sects which abound in this country, a very distinguished one is that of the Dumplers. It was founded by a German, who, disgusted with the world, retired to an agreeable solitude within fifty miles of Philadelphia, in order to be more at liberty to give himself up to contemplation. Curiosity brought several of his countrymen to visit his retreat; and by degrees his

his pious, simple, and peaceable manners induced them to settle near him, and they all formed a little colony, which they called Euphrates, in allusion to the Hebrews, who used to sing psalms on the borders of that river.

This little city forms a triangle, the outsides of which are bordered with mulberry and apple trees, planted with regularity. In the middle of the town is a very large orchard; and between the orchard and these ranges of trees are houses, built of wood, three stories high, where every Dumpler is left to enjoy the pleasures of his meditations without disturbance. These contemplative men do not amount to above five hundred in all; their territory is about 250 acres in extent, the boundaries of which are marked by a river, a piece of stagnated water, and a mountain covered with trees.

The men and women live in separate quarters of the city. They never see each other but at places of worship, nor are there any assemblies of any kind but for public business. Their life is taken up in labour, prayer, and sleep. Twice every day and night they are called forth from their cells, to attend divine service. Like the Methodists and Quakers, every individual among them possesses the right of preaching when he thinks himself inspired. The favourite subjects on which they

they love to difcourfe in their affemblies, are humility, temperance, chaftity, and the other Chriftian virtues. They never violate the reft of the Sabbath, which is fo much the delight of laborious as well as idle men. They admit a hell and a paradife; but reject the eternity of future punifhments. The doctrine of original fin is with them an impious blafphemy which they abhor, and in general every tenet cruel to man appears to them injurious to the Divinity. As they do not allow merit to any but voluntary works, they adminifter baptifm only to the adult. At the fame time they think baptifm fo effentially neceffary to falvation, that they imagine the fouls of Chriftians in another world are employed in converting thofe who have not died under the law of the gofpel.

Still more difinterefted than the Quakers, they never allow themfelves any law-fuits. One may cheat, rob, and abufe them, without ever being expofed to any retaliation, or even any complaint from them. Religion has the fame effect on them that philofophy had upon the Stoics; it makes them infenfible to every kind of infult.

Nothing can be plainer than their drefs. In winter, it confifts of a long white gown, from whence there hangs a hood to ferve inftead of a hat, a coarfe fhirt, thick fhoes, and very wide breeches. There is no great difference in summer, only that linen is used instead of woollen. The women are dressed much like the men except the breeches.

Their common food is only vegetable, not because it is unlawful to make use of any other, but because that kind of abstinence is looked upon as more conformable to the spirit of Christianity, which has an aversion for blood. Each individual follows with cheerfulness the branch of business allotted to him. The produce of all their labours is deposited into a common stock, in order to supply the necessities of every one. Besides the cultivation, manufactures, and all the arts necessary to the little society, which are thus produced by united industry, it affords a superfluous part for exchanges proportioned to the population.

Though the two sexes live separate at Euphrates, the Dumplers do not on that account foolishly renounce matrimony. But those who find themselves disposed to it leave the city, and form an establishment in the country, which is supported at the public expence. They repay this by the produce of their labours, which is all thrown into the public treasury, and their children are sent to be educated in the mother country. Without this wise privilege, the Dumplers would be nothing more than monks, and in
process

procefs of time would become either favages or libertines.

What is moft edifying, and at the fame time moft extraordinary, is, the harmony that fubfifts between all the fects eftablifhed in Penfylvania, notwithftanding the difference of their religious opinions. Tho' they are not all of the fame church, they all love and cherifh one another as children of the fame father. They have always continued to live like brothers, becaufe they had the liberty of thinking as men. It is to this delightful harmony that muft be attributed more particularly the rapid progrefs of the colony.

At the beginning of the year 1766 its population amounted to 150,000 white people. The number muft have been confiderably increafed from that period, fince it is doubled every fifteen years, according to Mr Franklin's calculations. There were ftill thirty thoufand blacks in the province, who met with lefs ill-ufage in this province than in the others, but who were ftill exceedingly unhappy. A circumftance, however, not eafily believed, is, that the fubjection of the negroes has not corrupted the morals of their mafters; their manners are ftill pure, and even auftere, in Penfylvania. Is this fingular advantage to be afcribed to the climate, the laws, the religion, the emulation conftantly fubfifting between the different fects,

or

or to some other particular cause? Let the reader determine this question.

The Pensylvanians are in general well made, and their women of an agreeable figure. As they sooner become mothers than in Europe, they sooner cease breeding. If the heat of the climate seems on the one hand to hasten the operations of nature, its inconstancy weakens them on the other. There is no place where the temperature of the sky is more uncertain, for it sometimes changes five of six times in the same day.

As, however, these varieties neither have any dangerous influence upon the vegetables, nor destroy the harvests, there is a constant plenty, and an universal appearance of ease. The œconomy which is so particularly attended to in Pensylvania does not prevent both sexes from being well clothed; and their food is still preferable in its kind to their clothing. The families, whose circumstances are the least easy, have all of them bread, meat, cyder, beer, and rum. A very great number are able to afford to drink constantly French and Spanish wines, punch, and even liquors of a higher price. The abuse of these strong drinks is less frequent than in other places, but is not without example.

The pleasing view of this abundance is never disturbed by the melancholy sight of poverty.

poverty. There are no poor in all Penfylvania. All thofe whofe birth or fortune have left them without refources, are fuitably provided for out of the public treafury. The fpirit of benevolence is carried ftill further, and is extended even to the moft engaging hofpitality. A traveller is welcome to ftop in any place, without the apprehenfions of giving the leaft uneafy fenfation, except that of regret for his departure.

The happinefs of the colony is not difturbed by the oppreffive burden of taxes. In 1766, they did not amount to more than 12,256*l*. 2*s*. 6*d*. Moft of them, even thofe that were defigned to repair the damages of war, were to ceafe in 1772. If the people did not experience this alleviation at that period, it was owing to the eruptions of the favages, which had occafioned extraordinary expences.

The Penfylvanians, happy poffeffors and peaceable tenants of a country that ufually renders them twenty or thirty fold for whatever they lay out upon it, are not reftrained by fear from the propagation of their fpecies. There is hardly an unmarried perfon to be met with in the country. Marriage is only the more happy and the more reverenced for it. The freedom as well as the fanctity of it depends upon the choice of the parties: they chufe the lawyer and prieft rather as witneffes nesses, than ministers, of the engagement. Whenever two lovers meet with any opposition, they go off on horseback together. The man gets behind his mistress; and in this situation they present themselves before the magistrate, where the girl declares she has run away with her lover, and that they are come to be married. So solemn an avowal cannot be rejected, nor has any person a right to give them any molestation. In all other cases, paternal athority is excessive. The head of a family, whose affairs are involved, is allowed to engage his children to his creditors; a punishment, one should imagine, very sufficient to induce a fond father to attend to his affairs. A man grown up acquits in one year's service a debt of 5*l.* and children under twelve years of age are obliged to serve till they are one and twenty, to pay one of 6*l.* This is an image of the old patriarchal manners of the East.

Though there are several villages, and even some cities, in the colony, most of the inhabitants may be said to live separately, as it were, within their families. Every proprietor of land has his house in the midst of a large plantation entirely surrounded with quickset hedges. Of course each parish is near twelve or fifteen leagues in circumference. This distance of the churches makes the ceremonies of religion have little effect,

and

and ſtill leſs influence. Children are not baptized till a few months, and ſometimes not till a year or two, after their birth.

All the pomp of religion ſeems reſerved for the laſt honours man receives before he is ſhut up in the grave for ever. As ſoon as any one is dead in the country, the neareſt neighbours have notice given them of the day of burial. Theſe ſpread it in the habitations next to theirs, and within a few hours the news is thus conveyed to a diſtance. Every family ſends at leaſt one perſon to attend the funeral. As they come in they are preſented with punch and cake. When the aſſembly is complete, the corpſe is carried to the burying ground belonging to his ſect; or, if that ſhould be at too great a diſtance, into one of the fields belonging to the family. There is generally a train of four or five hundred perſons on horſeback, who obſerve a continual ſilence, and have all the external appearance ſuited to the melancholy nature of the ceremony. One ſingular circumſtance is, that the Penſylvanians, who are the greateſt enemies to parade during their lives, ſeem to forget this character of modeſty at their deaths. They all are deſirous that the poor remains of their ſhort lives ſhould be attended with a funeral pomp ſuited to their rank or fortune.

It is a general obſervation, that plain and
vir-

virtuous nations, even savage and poor ones, are remarkably attached to the care of their burials. The reason of it is, that they look upon these last honours as duties of the survivors, and the duties themselves as so many distinct proofs of that principle of love which is very strong in private families whilst they are in a state nearest to that of nature. It is not the dying man himself who exacts these honours; it is his parents, his wife, his children, who voluntarily pay them to the ashes of a husband and father that has deserved to be lamented. These ceremonies have always more numerous attendants in small societies than in larger ones; because, though there are fewer families upon the whole, the number of individuals there is much larger, and all the ties that connect them with each other are much stronger. This kind of intimate union has been the reason why so many small nations have overcome larger ones; it drove Xerxes and the Persians out of Greece, and it will some time or other expel the French out of Corsica.

But from whence does Pensylvania draw the materials for her own consumption, and in what manner does she contrive to be abundantly furnished with them? With the flax and hemp that are produced at home, and the cotton she procures from South America, she fabricates a great quantity of ordinary linens; and with the wool that comes from Europe she manufactures many coarse cloths. Whatever her own industry is not able to furnish, she purchases with the produce of her territory. Her ships carry over to the British, French, Dutch, and Danish islands, biscuit, flour, butter, cheese, tallow, vegetables, fruits, salt meat, cyder, beer, and all sorts of wood for building. The cotton, sugar, coffee, brandy, and money, they receive in exchange, are so many materials for a fresh commerce with the mother country, and with other European nations as well as with other colonies. The Azores, Madeira, the Canaries, Spain, and Portugal, open an advantageous market to the corn and wood of Pensylvania, which they purchase with wine and piastres. The mother country receives from Pensylvania iron, flax, leather, furs, linseed oil, masts and yards; for which it returns thread, wool, fine cloths, tea, Irish and India linens, hard-ware, and other articles of luxury or necessity. As these, however, amount to a much greater sum than what it buys, Britain may be considered as a gulph in which all the metals Pensylvania has drawn from the other parts of the world are sunk again. In 1723, Britain sent over goods to Pensylvania only to the value of 10,937*l*. 10*s*. at present she furnishes to the amount of 437,500*l*. This sum is too considersiderable for the colonists to be able to pay it, even in depriving themselves of all the gold they draw from other markets; and this inability must continue as long as the improvement of their cultures shall require more considerable advances than their produce yields. Other colonies which enjoy almost exclusively some branches of trade, such as rice, tobacco, and indigo, must have grown rich very rapidly. Pensylvania, whose riches are founded on agriculture and the increase of her flocks, will acquire them more gradually; but her prosperity will be fixed upon a more firm and permanent basis.

If any circumstance can retard the progress of the colony, it must be the irregular manner in which the plantations are formed. Penn's family, who are the proprietors of all the lands, grant them indiscriminately in all parts, and in as large a proportion as they are required, provided they are paid 6*l.* 11 *s.* 3 *d.* for each hundred acres, and that the purchasers agree to give an annual rent of about one halfpenny. The consequence of this is, that the province wants that sort of connection which is necessary in all things, and that the scattered inhabitants easily become the prey of the most insignificant enemy that will venture to attack them.

The habitations are cleared in different ways in the colony. Sometimes a huntsman will

will settle in the midſt of a foreſt, or quite cloſe to it. His neareſt neighbours aſſiſt him in cutting down trees, and heaping them up one over another: and this conſtitutes a houſe. Around this ſpot he cultivates, without any aſſiſtance, a garden or a field, ſufficient to ſubſiſt himſelf and his family.

A few years after the firſt labours were finiſhed, ſome more active and richer men arrived from the mother country. They paid the huntſman for his pains, and agreed with the proprietors of the provinces for ſome lands that had not been paid for. They built more commodious habitations, and cleared a greater extent of territory.

At length ſome Germans, who came into the new world from inclination, or were driven into it by perſecution, completed theſe ſettlements that were as yet unfiniſhed. The firſt and ſecond order of planters removed their induſtry into other parts, with a more conſiderable ſtock for carrying on their cultures than they had at firſt.

The annual exports of Penſylvania may be valued at 25,000 tons. It receives four hundred ſhips, and fits out about an equal number. They all, or almoſt all, come into PHILADELPHIA, which is the capital, from whence they are alſo diſpatched.

This famous city, whoſe very name recalls every humane feeling, is ſituated at the conflux of the Delaware and the Schuylkill, about 120 miles from the sea. Penn, who destined it for the metropolis of a great empire, designed it to be one mile in breadth, and two in length between the rivers; but its population has proved insufficient to cover this extent of ground. Hitherto they have built only upon the banks of the Delaware; but without giving up the ideas of the legislator, or deviating from his plan. These precautions are highly proper: Philadelphia must become the most considerable city of America, because it is impossible that the colony should not improve greatly, and its productions must pass through the harbour of the capital before they arrive at the sea. The streets of Philadelphia, which are all regular, are in general fifty feet broad; the two principal ones are a hundred. On each side of them, there are foot-paths, guarded by posts placed at different distances. The houses, each of which has its garden and orchard, are commonly two stories high; and are built either of brick, or of a kind of soft stone, which grows hard by being exposed to the air. Till very lately the walls had but little thickness, because they were only to be covered with a very light kind of wood. Since the discovery of slate quarries, the walls have acquired a solidity proportioned to the weight of the new roofs. The present buildings have received

ceived an additional decoration from a kind of marble of different colours, which is found about a mile out of the town. Of this they make tables, chimney-pieces, and other household furniture: besides which it is become a pretty considerable object of commerce with the greatest part of America.

These valuable materials could not have been commonly found in the houses, if they had not been lavished in the churches. Every sect has its own church, and some of them have several.

The town-house is a building held in as much veneration, though not so much frequented, as the churches. It is constructed in the most sumptuous magnificence. It is there that the legislators of the colony assemble every year, and more frequently if necessary, to settle every thing relative to public business; the whole of which is submitted to the authority of the nation in the persons of its representatives. Next to the town-house is a most elegant library, which owes its existence to the care of the learned Doctor Franklin. In it are found the best English, French, and Latin authors. It is only open to the public on Saturdays. Those who have founded it have a free access to it the whole year. The rest pay a trifle for the loan of the books, and a forfeit if they are not returned in due time. This little fund constantly accumulating is appropriated to the increase of the library; to which have been lately added, in order to make it more useful, some mathematical and philosophical instruments, with a very fine cabinet of natural history.

The college, which is intended to prepare the mind for the attainment of all the sciences, was founded in 1749. At first, it only initiated the youth in the Belles Lettres. In 1764 a class of medicine was established there. Knowledge of every kind and adepts in the sciences will increase in proportion as the lands, which are become their patrimony, shall yield a greater produce. If ever despotism, superstition, or war, should plunge Europe again into that state of barbarism from whence philosophy and the arts have drawn it, the sacred fire will be kept alive in Philadelphia, and come from thence to enlighten the world. This city is amply supplied with every assistance human nature can require, and with all the resources industry can make use of. Its keys, the principal of which is two hundred feet wide, present a suite of convenient warehouses and recesses ingeniously contrived for ship-building. Ships of five hundred tons may land there without any difficulty, except in the times of frost. There they load the merchandise which has either come down the Schuylkill and Delaware, or

along

or along roads better than are to be met with in moſt parts of Europe. Police has made a greater progreſs in this part of the new world, than among the moſt ancient nations of the old. It is impoſſible to determine pre- ciſely the population of Philadelphia, as the bills of mortality are not kept with any ex- actneſs, and there are ſeveral ſects who do not chriſten their children. It appears a fact, however, that in 1766 it contained twenty thouſand inhabitants. As moſt of them are employed in the ſale of the productions of the colony, and in ſupplying it with what they draw from abroad, it is impoſſible that their fortunes ſhould not be very conſider- able; and they muſt increaſe ſtill further, in proportion as the cultivation advances in a country where hitherto not above one ſixth of the land has been cleared.

Philadelphia, as well as Newcaſtle and the other cities of Penſylvania, is entirely open. The whole country is equally without de- fence. This is a neceſſary conſequence of the principles of the Quakers, who have al- ways maintained the principal influence in the public deliberations, though they do not form above one third part of the population of the colony. Theſe ſectaries cannot be too much favoured on account of their mo- deſty, probity, love of labour, and benevo- lence. One might, perhaps, be tempted to accuse their legislation of imprudence and temerity.

When they established that civil liberty which protects one citizen from another, ought not the founders of the colony to have taken some pains for the maintenance of political liberty also, which protects one state from the encroachments of another? The authority which exerts itself to maintain peace and good order at home, seems to have done nothing if it has not prevented invasion from abroad. To pretend that the colony would never have any enemies, was to suppose the world peopled with Quakers. It was encouraging the strong to fall upon the weak, leaving the lamb to the mercy of the wolf, and giving up all the country to the oppressive yoke of the first tyrant who should think proper to subdue it.

But, on the other hand, how shall we reconcile the strictness of the gospel-maxims, by which the Quakers are literally governed, with that appearance of force, either for offence or defence, which puts all Christian nations in a continual state of war with each other? Besides, what could the French or the Spaniards do if they were to enter Pensylvania sword in hand? Unless they should destroy in one night or in one day all the inhabitants of that fortunate region, they would not be able to cut off the race of those mild

and

and charitable men. Violence has its boundaries in its very excess; it consumes and extinguishes itself, as the fire in the ashes that feed it. But virtue, when guided by humanity and brotherly love, reanimates itself as the tree under the edge of the pruning knife. Wicked men stand in need of numbers to execute their sanguinary projects. But the just man, or the Quaker, requires only a brother from whom he may receive, or to whom he may give, assistance. Let, then, the warlike nations, people who are either slaves or tyrants, go into Pensylvania: there they will find all avenues open to them, all property at their disposal; not a single soldier, but numbers of merchants and farmers. But if they are tormented, restrained, or oppressed, they will fly, and leave their lands uncultivated, their manufactures destroyed, and their warehouses empty. They will go and cultivate, and spread population in some new land; they will go round the world, and expire in their progress rather than turn their arms against their pursuers, or submit to bear their yoke. Their enemies will have acquired nothing but the hatred of mankind and the curses of posterity.

It is upon this prospect and on this foresight, that the Pensylvanians have founded the opinion of their future security. At present they have nothing to fear from behind,
since

since the French have lost Canada; and the flanks of the colony are sufficiently covered by the British settlements. As for the rest, as they do not see that the most warlike states are the most durable; or that mistrust, which is always awake, makes them rest in greater quiet; or that there is any kind of satisfaction in the enjoyment of that which is held with so much fear; they live for the present moment, without any thought of a future day. Perhaps, too, they may think themselves secured by those very precautions that are taken in the colonies that surround them. One of the barriers or bulwarks that preserves Pensylvania from a maritime invasion to which it is exposed, is Virginia.

CHAP. II.

Of Virginia and Maryland.

1 *Wretched state of Virginia at its first settlement.*

VIRGINIA, which was intended to denote all that extensive space which the English proposed to occupy in the continent of North America, is at present confined within much narrower limits. It now comprehends only that country which is bounded to the north by Maryland, to the south by Carolina, to the

the weſt by the Apalachian mountains, and to the eaſt by the ocean. This ſpace contains two hundred and forty miles in length, and two hundred in breadth.

It was in 1606 that the Engliſh firſt landed at Virginia; and their firſt ſettlement was James-Town. Unfortunately the firſt object that preſented itſelf to them was a rivulet, which, iſſuing from a ſand-bank, drew after it a quantity of talc, which glittered at the bottom of a clear and running water. In an age when gold and ſilver mines were the only objects of mens reſearches, this deſpicable ſubſtance was immediately taken for ſilver. Every other labour was inſtantly ſuſpended to acquire it. And the illuſion was ſo complete, that two ſhips, which had arrived there with neceſſaries, were ſent home ſo fully freighted with theſe imaginary riches, that there ſcarce remained any room for a few furs. As long as the infatuation laſted, the coloniſts diſdained to employ themſelves in clearing the lands; ſo that a dreadful famine was at laſt the conſequence of this fooliſh pride. Sixty men only remained alive out of five hundred that had come from Europe. Theſe few, having only a fortnight's proviſion left, were upon the point of embarking for Newfoundland, when lord Delaware arrived there with three ſhips, a freſh colony, and ſupplies of all kinds.

Hiſtory

History has described this nobleman to us as a man whose genius raised him above the common prejudices of the times. His disinterestedness was equal to his knowledge. In accepting the government of the colony, which was still in its infancy, his only motives had been to gratify the inclination a virtuous mind has to do good, and to secure the esteem of posterity, which is the second reward of that generosity that devotes itself totally to the service of the public. As soon as he appeared, the knowledge of his character procured him universal respect. He began by endeavouring to reconcile the wretched colonists to their fatal country, to comfort them in their sufferings, to make them hope for a speedy conclusion of them. After this, joining the firmness of an enlightened magistrate to the tenderness of a good father, he taught them how to direct their labours to an useful end. For the misfortune of the reviving colony, Delaware's declining health soon obliged him to return to Europe; but he never lost sight of his favourite colonists, nor ever failed to make use of all his credit and interest at court to support them. The colony, however, made but little progress; a circumstance that was attributed to the oppression of exclusive privileges. The company which exercised them was dissolved upon Charles I.'s accession to the throne; and from

from that time Virginia was under the immediate direction of the crown, which exacted no more than a rent of 2s. upon every hundred acres that were cultivated.

Till this moment the colonists had known no true enjoyment of property. Every individual wandered where chance directed him, or fixed himself in the place he liked best, without consulting any titles or agreements. At length, boundaries were ascertained; and those who had been so long wanderers, now become citizens, had determined limits to their plantations. The establishment of this first law of society changed the appearance of every thing. New buildings arose on all sides, and were surrounded by fresh cultivations. This activity drew great numbers of enterprising men over to Virginia, who came in search either of fortune, or of liberty which is the only compensation for the want of it. The memorable troubles that produced a change in the constitution of England added to these a multitude of Royalists, who went there with a resolution to wait with Berkley, the governor of the colony, who was also attached to king Charles, the decision of that deserted mornarch's fate. Berkley still continued to protect them, even after the king's death; but some of the inhabitants, either seduced or intimidated, and seconded by the approach of a powerful fleet, delivered up the colony

colony to the Protector. If the governor was compelled to follow the stream against his will, he was at least, among those whom Charles had honoured with posts of confidence and rank, the last who submitted to Cromwell, and the first who shook off his yoke. This brave man was sinking under the oppression of the times, when the voice of the people recalled him to the place which his successor's death had left vacant; but far from yielding to these flattering solicitations, he declared that he never would serve any but the legitimate heirs of the dethroned monarch. Such an example of magnanimity, at a time when there were no hopes of the restoration of the royal family, made such an impression upon the minds of the people, that Charles II. was proclaimed in Virginia before he had been proclaimed in England.

The colony did not, however, receive all the benefit from such a step which might naturally have been expected from it. Whilst the court, on one hand, granted to rapacious men of family exorbitant privileges, which swallowed up the properties of several obscure colonists; the parliament, on the other, laid excessive taxes upon both the exports from and imports to Virginia. This double oppression drained all the resources and dispelled all the hopes of the colony; and, to complete its misfortune, the savages, who had
never

never been sufficiently careffed, took that opportunity to renew their incurfions with a fpirit and uniformity of defign that had never been yet known,

Such a complication of misfortunes drove the Virginians to defpair. Berkley, who had fo long been their idol, was accufed of wanting fortitude to refift the oppreffions of the mother country, and activity to repel the irruptions of the favages. The eyes of all were immediately fixed upon Bacon, a young officer, full of vivacity, eloquence, and intrepidity, of an infinuating difpofition and an agreeable perfon. They chofe him for their general in an irregular and tumultuous manner. Though his military fucceffes might have juftified this prepoffeffion of the licentious multitude, yet this did not prevent the governor from declaring Bacon a traitor to his country. A fentence fo fevere, and which was imprudent at the time, determined Bacon to affume a power by force which he had exercifed peaceably and without oppofition for fix months. His death put a ftop to all his projects. The malecontents, difunited by the death of their chief, and intimidated by the troops which were coming from Europe, were induced to fue for pardon, which was readily granted them. The rebellion, therefore, was attended with no bad confequences. Mercy infured obedience; and fince
that

that remarkable crisis the history of Virginia has been confined to the account of its plantations.

2. *Administration of Virginia.*

This great establishment was governed at the beginning by persons placed at the head of it by the company. Virginia afterwards attracted the attention of the mother country; which in 1620 gave it a regular form of government, composed of a chief, a council, and deputies from each county; to whose united care the interests of the province were committed. At first, the council and representatives of the people used to meet in the same room: but in 1689 they divided, and had each their separate chamber, in imitation of the parliament of England. This custom has been continued ever since.

The governor, who is always appointed by the king, and for an unlimited period, has the sole disposal of the regular troops, the militia, and of all military employments, as well as the power of approving or rejecting whatever laws are proposed by the general assembly. Besides this, with the concurrence of the council, to which he leaves very little power in other matters, he may either prorogue or entirely dissolve this kind of parliament:

ment: he chufes all magiftrates, and all the collectors of the revenue; he alienates the unoccupied lands in a manner fuitable to the eftablifhed forms, and difpofes of the public treafure. So many prerogatives, which lead on to ufurpation, render government more arbitrary at Virginia than it is in the more northern colonies: they frequently open the door to oppreffion.

The council is compofed of twelve members, created either by letters patent, or by particular order from the king. When there happen to be lefs than nine in the country, the governor chufes three out of the principal inhabitants to make up the number. They form a kind of upper-houfe, and are at the fame time to affift the adminiftration, and to counteract tyranny. They have alfo the power of rejecting all acts paffed in the lower houfe. The falaries of the whole body amount to no more than 384*l*. 10*s*. 10¼*d*.

Virginia is divided into 25 counties, each of which fends two deputies. James-town and the college have each of them feparately the right of naming one, which make up in all 52. Every inhabitant poffeffed of a freehold, except only women and minors, has the right of election, and that of being elected. Though there is no time fixed by law for holding the general affembly, it commonly meets either once a year, or once in

VOL. I.   N   every

every two years; and the meeting is very feldom deferred till three. The frequency of thefe meetings is infallibly kept up by the precaution of granting fupplies only for a fhort time. All acts paffed in the two houfes muft be fent over to the fovereign, to receive his fanction; but till that returns, they are always in force, when they have been approved by the governor.

The public revenues of Virginia are collected from different fources, and appropriated in different manners. The tax of 1 *s*. 11½ *d*. upon every quintal of tobacco; that of 14 *s*. 9 *d*. per ton, which every veffel full or empty is obliged to pay at its return from a voyage; that of 9 *s*. 10 *d*. a-head exacted from all paffengers, flaves as well as freemen, upon their arrival in the colony; the penalties and forfeitures appointed by different acts of the province; the duty upon both the lands and perfonal eftates of thofe who leave no legitimate heir; thefe different articles, which together amount to 3,062 *l*. 10 *s*. are to be employed in the current expences of the colony, according to the direction of the governor and the council. The general affembly has nothing more to do in this matter but to audit the accounts.

This affembly, however, has referved to itfelf the fole difpofition of the funds raifed for extraordinary fervices. Thefe arife from a duty of entrance upon strong liquors, from one of 19 *s*. 8¼ *d*. upon every slave, and one of about 14 *s*. 9 *d*. upon every servant, not an Englishman, that enters the colony. A revenue of this nature must be extremely variable; but in general it is pretty considerable, and has been usually well administered.

Besides these taxes which are paid in money, there are others paid in kind. They are a sort of a triple poll-tax on the article of tobacco, which the white women only are exempted from. The first is raised by order of the general assembly, for the purpose of paying the expences of its meeting, for that of the militia, and for some other national exigences. The second, which is called provincial, is imposed by the justices of the peace in each county for its particular uses. The third is parochial, raised by the chief persons of the community, upon every thing that has more or less connection with the established form of worship.

In the beginning justice was administered with that kind of disinterestedness which was itself the security for the equity observed in it. One single court had the cognizance of all causes, and used to decide them in a few days, leaving only an appeal to the general assembly, which was not less diligent in terminating them. So good a system did not continue long: in 1692 all the statutes and formalities of the mother country were adopted, and all the chicanery of it was introduced along with them. Since that time every county has its diſtinct tribunal, compoſed of a ſheriff, his under-officers, and juries. From theſe courts all cauſes are carried to the council, where the governor preſides, who has the power of determining finally in all concerns as far as about 295 *l.* If the ſums contended for are more conſiderable, the conteſt may be referred to the king: in all criminal matters the council pronounces without appeal; not that the life of a citizen is of leſs conſequence than his property, but becauſe the application of the law is much eaſier in criminal than in civil cauſes. The governor has the right of pardoning in all caſes but thoſe of wilful murder and high treaſon, and even in theſe he may ſuſpend the execution of the ſentence till he has ſent to know the king's pleaſure.

With reſpect to religion, the inhabitants not only began themſelves by profeſſing that of the church of England; but, in 1642, the aſſembly paſſed a decree, which indirectly excluded from the province all thoſe who ſhould not be of this communion. The neceſſity of peopling the country ſoon occaſioned the repeal of this law, which was rather of a hierarchal than of a religious nature. A toleration granted ſo late, and evidently with

re-

reluctance, produced no great effect. Only five non-conformist churches were added to the colony, one of which consisted of Presbyterians, three of Quakers, and one of French refugees.

The mother church has 39 parishes. Every parish chuses its minister; who must, however, be approved of by the governor before he takes possession. In some parishes, he is paid in land, and furnished with all the necessary instruments for cultivating it; in others, his salary is 16,000 pounds weight of tobacco. Besides this, he receives either about 4 *s*. 11 *d*. or fifty pounds of tobacco, for every marriage; and 1 *l*. 19 *s*. 4½ *d*. or four hundred pounds of tobacco, for every funeral sermon, which he is obliged to make over the grave of every free man. With all these advantages, most of the clergy are not contented, because they may be deprived of their benefices by those who conferred them.

At first the colony was inhabited only by men; soon after, they grew desirous of sharing the sweets of their situation with female companions. In the beginning they gave 98 *l*. 8 *s*. 9 *d*. for every young person that was brought them, from whom they required no other dowry than a certificate of virtue. When the salubrity and fertility of the climate were ascertained, whole families, and even some of respectable condition, went over to settle in Virginia. In time they increased to such a degree, that in 1703 there were already 66,606 white people in the colony. If since that time they have not increased above a sixth, it must be attributed to a pretty considerable emigration occasioned by the arrival of the blacks.

The first of these slaves were brought into Virginia by a Dutch ship in 1621. Their number was not considerable at first; but the increase of them has been so prodigious since the beginning of this century, that there are at present 110,000 negroes in the colony; which occasions a double loss to mankind, first in exhausting the population of Africa, and secondly in preventing that of the Europeans in America.

Virginia has neither fortified places nor regular troops; they would be useless in a province, which from its situation and the nature of its productions is protected both from foreign invasions, and from the incursions of the savages wandering about this vast continent, who have long been too weak to attack it. The militia, which is composed of all the free-men from sixteen to sixty years of age, is sufficient to keep the slaves in order. Every county reviews all its troops once, and the separate companies three or four times a year. Upon the least alarm given in any particular part of the country, all the forces in it march. If they are out more than two days, they receive pay; if not, it is reckoned a part of their stated service. Such is the government of Virginia, and such is very nearly that of Maryland; which, after having been included in this colony, was separated from it for reasons which must be explained.

3. *Maryland is detached from Virginia.*

CHARLES the First, far from having any aversion for the Catholics, had some reason to protect them, from the zeal, which, in hopes of being tolerated, they had shewn for his interest. But when the accusation of being favourable to popery had alienated the minds of the people from that weak prince, whose chief aim was to establish a despotic government, he was obliged to give the Catholics up to the rigour of the laws enacted against them by Henry the Eighth. These circumstances induced lord Baltimore to seek an asylum in Virginia, where he might be indulged in a liberty of conscience. As he found there no toleration for an exclusive faith which was itself intolerant, he formed the design of a new settlement in that uninhabited part of the country which lay between the river of Potowmack and Pensylvania. His death, which happened soon after he had obtained powers from the crown for peopling this land, put a stop to the project for that time; but it was resumed, from the same religious motives, by his son. This young nobleman left England in the year 1633, with two hundred Roman Catholics, most of them of good families. The education they had received, the cause of religion for which they left their country, and the fortune which their leader promised them, prevented those disturbances which are but too common in infant settlements. The neighbouring savages, prevailed upon by mildness and acts of beneficence, concurred with eagerness to assist the new colonists in forming their settlement. With this unexpected help these fortunate persons, attached to each other by the same principles of religion, and directed by the prudent counsels of their chief, applied themselves unanimously to every kind of useful labour: the view of the peace and happiness they enjoyed, invited among them a number of men who were persecuted either for the same religion, or for different opinions.

The Catholics of Maryland gave up at length the intolerant principles, of which they themselves had been the victims after having first set the example of them, and opened the doors of their colony to all sects of what religious principles soever. Baltimore

more alfo granted the moft extenfive civil liberty to every ftranger who chofe to purchafe lands in his new colony, the government of which was modelled upon that of the mother country.

Thefe wife and generous precautions, however, did not fecure the governor, at the time of the fubverfion of the monarchy, from lofing all the rights and conceffions that he had obtained. Deprived of his poffeffions by Cromwell, he was reftored to them by Charles II. after which they were again difputed with him. Tho' he was perfectly clear from any reproach of mal-adminiftration; and though he was extremely zealous for the Tramontane doctrines, and much attached to the intereft of the Stuarts; yet he had the mortification of finding the legality of his charter attacked under the arbitrary reign of James II. and of being obliged to maintain an action at law for the jurifdiction of a province which had been ceded to him by the crown, and which he himfelf had peopled. This prince, whofe misfortune it had always been never to have known his friends from his foes, and who had alfo the ridiculous pride to think that regal authority was fufficient to juftify every act of violence, was preparing a fecond time to deprive Baltimore, of what had been given him by two kings, his father and his brother; when he

was

was himself removed from the throne which he filled so ill. The successor of this weak despotic prince terminated this contest, which had arisen before his accession to the crown, in a manner worthy of his political character. He left the Baltimores in possession of their revenues, but deprived them of their authority; which, however, they likewise recovered, upon becoming members of the church of England.

The province is at present divided into eleven counties, and inhabited by 40,000 white men and 60,000 blacks. It is governed by a chief, who is named by the proprietor, and by a council and two deputies chosen in each county. The governor, like the king in the other colonies, has a negative voice in all acts proposed by the assembly; that is to say, the right of rejecting them.

4. *Virginia and Maryland cultivate the same productions.*

IF Maryland were re-united to Virginia, as their common interest seems to require, no difference could be found between the two settlements. They are situated between Pensylvania and Carolina, and occupy the great space that extends from the sea to the Apalachian mountains. The air, which is damp on the coast, becomes light, pure, and subtle,

as

as one approaches the mountains. The fpring and autumn months are of an excellent temperature: in fummer there are fome days exceffively hot, and in winter fome extremely cold; but neither of thefe exceffes lafts above a week at a time. The moft difagreeable circumftance in the climate is the abundance of naufeous infects that are found there.

All the domeftic animals multiply prodigioufly; and all forts of fruits, trees, and vegetables, fucceed there extremely well. There is the beft corn in all America. The foil, which is rich and fertile in the low lands, is always good, even in thofe places where it becomes more fandy; more irregular than it is defcribed by fome travellers, but tolerably even till one comes near the mountains.

From thefe refervoirs an incredible number of rivers flow, moft of which are feparated only by an interval of five or fix miles. Befides the fertility which thefe waters impart to the country they pafs through, they alfo make it infinitely more convenient for trade than any other part of the new world, from facilitating the communications.

Moft of thefe rivers have a very extenfive inland navigation for merchant-fhips, and fome of them for men of war. One may go near two hundred miles up the Potowmack; above eighty up the James, the York, and the
Ra-

Rapahannock; and, upon the other rivers, to a distance that varies according as the cataracts are more or less distant from their mouths. All these navigable canals, formed by nature, meet in the bay of Chesapeak, which has from seven to nine fathom water both at its entrance and in its whole extent. It reaches above two hundred miles in the inland parts of the country, and is about twelve miles in its mean breadth. Tho' it is full of small islands, most of them covered with wood, it is by no means dangerous; and so large, that all the ships in the universe might ride there with ease.

So uncommon an advantage has prevented the formation of any large towns in the two colonies; and accordingly the inhabitants, who were assured that the ships would come up to their warehouses, and that they might embark their commodities without going from their own houses, have dispersed themselves upon the borders of the several rivers. In this situation, they found all the pleasures of a rural life, united to all the ease that trade brings into cities; they found the facility of extending their cultivation in a country that had no bounds, united to all the assistance which the fertilization of the lands receives from commerce. But the mother country suffered a double inconvenience from this dispersion of the colonists: first, because her

her sailors were longer absent, by being obliged to collect their cargoes from these scattered habitations; and secondly, because their ships are exposed to injury from those dangerous insects, which in the months of June and July infest all the rivers of this distant region. The ministry has therefore neglected no means of engaging the colonists to establish staples for the reception of their commodities. The constraint of the laws has not had more effect than persuasion. At length, a few years ago, forts were ordered to be built at the entrance of every river, to protect the loading and unloading of the ships. If this project had not failed in the execution from the want of a sufficient fund, it is probable that the inhabitants would have collected imperceptibly round each of these fortresses. But it may still be questioned whether this circumstance would not have proved fatal to population, and whether agriculture might not have lost as much as commerce would have gained by it.

Be this as it may, it is certain that there are but two towns at present of any kind of note in the two colonies. Even those which are the seat of government are of no great importance. Williamsburgh the capital of Virginia, and Annapolis that of Maryland, the first risen upon the ruins of James-town, the other upon those of St Mary, are neither
of

of them superior to one of our common villages.

As, in all human affairs, every good is attended with some kind of evil; so it has happened, that the increase of habitations, by retarding the population of towns, has prevented any artists or manufacturers from being formed in either of the provinces. With all the materials necessary to supply them with most of their wants, and even with several of their conveniences, they are still obliged to draw from Europe their cloths, linens, hats, hardware, and even furniture of the most ordinary kind.

These numerous and general expences have exhausted the inhabitants; besides which, they have vied with each other in displaying every kind of luxury before all the British merchants who visit their plantations from motives of commercial interest. By these means, they have run so much in debt with the mother country, that many of them have been obliged to sell their lands; or, in order still to keep possession of them, to mortgage them at an usurious interest of eight or nine *per cent.*

It will be no easy matter for the two provinces ever to emerge from this desperate state. Their navy does not amount to above a thousand tons; and all they send to the Carribbee islands in corn, cattle, and planks,

with

with all they expedite for Europe in hemp, flax, leather, peltry, and walnut-tree or cedar wood, does not bring them a return of more than 43,750 *l.* The only resource they have left is in tobacco.

5. *Of the Tobacco-trade.*

TOBACCO is a sharp, caustic, and even venomous plant, which has been formerly of great repute, and is still used in medicine. Every body is acquainted with the general consumption made of it, by chewing, smoking, or taking snuff. It was discovered in the year 1520 by the Spaniards, who found it first in the Jucatan, a large peninsula in the gulph of Mexico, from whence it was carried into the neighbouring islands. Soon after, the use of it became a matter of dispute among the learned, which the ignorant also took a part in; and thus tobacco acquired some reputation. By degrees fashion and custom have greatly extended its consumption in all parts of the known world. It is at present cultivated with more or less success in Europe, Asia, Africa, and several parts of America.

The stem of this plant is straight, hairy, and viscous; and its leaves are thick, flabby, and of a pale-green colour. They are larger at the bottom than at the summit of the plant. It requires a soil of a good consistence; but rich,

even,

even, deep, and not too much expofed to inundations. A virgin foil is very fit for this vegetable, which requires a great deal of fap.

The feeds of the tobacco are fown in layers. When it has grown to the height of two inches, and has got at leaft half a dozen leaves, it is gently pulled up in damp weather, and tranfplanted with great care into a well-prepared foil, where the plants are placed at the diftance of three feet from each other. When they are put into the ground with thefe precautions, their leaves do not fuffer the leaft injury; and all their vigour is renewed in four and twenty hours.

The cultivation of tobacco requires continual attention. The weeds which gather about it muft be plucked up; the head of it muft be cut off when it is the fize of two feet and a half, to prevent it from growing too high; it muft be ftripped of all fprouting fuckers; the leaves which grow too low down upon the ftem, thofe that are in the leaft inclined to decay, and thofe which the infects have touched, muft all be removed, and their number reduced to eight or ten at moft. A fingle induftrious man is able to take care of two thoufand five hundred plants, which ought to yield one thoufand weight of tobacco. It is left about four months in the ground. As it advances to maturity, the pleafant and lively green colour

lour of its leaves is changed into a darker hue; the leaves are also curved, and the smell they exhale is increased, and extends to a greater distance. The plant is then ripe, and must be cut.

The plants, when collected, are laid in heaps upon the same ground that produced them, where they are left to exsude only for one night. The next day they are laid up in warehouses, constructed in such a manner that the air may have free access to them on all sides. Here they are left separately suspended as long a time as is necessary to dry them well. They are then spread upon hurdles, and well covered over; where they ferment for a week or two. At last they are stripped of their leaves, which are either put into barrels, or made up into rolls. The other methods of preparing the plant, which vary according to the different tastes of the several nations that use it, have nothing to do with its cultivation.

Of all the countries in which tobacco has been planted, there is none where it has answered so well as in Maryland and Virginia. As it was the only occupation of the first planters, they often cultivated much more than they could find a sale for. They were then obliged to stop the growth of the plantations in Virginia, and to burn a certain number of plants in every habitation throughout Maryland. But in procefs of time the ufes of this herb became fo general, that they have been obliged to increafe the number both of the whites and blacks who are employed in preparing it. At prefent each of the colonies furnifhes nearly an equal quantity. That from Virginia, which is the mildeft, the moft perfumed, and the deareft, is confumed in England and in the fouthern parts of Europe. That of Maryland is fitter for the northern climates, from its cheapnefs, and even from its coarfenefs, which makes it better adapted to lefs delicate organs.

As navigation has not yet made the fame progrefs in thefe provinces as in the reft of North America, the tobacco is commonly tranfported in the fhips of the mother country. They are very often three, four, and even fix months in completing their cargo. This delay arifes from feveral very evident caufes. Firft, as there are no magazines or general receptacles for the tobacco, it is neceffary to go and fetch it from the feveral plantations. Secondly, few planters are able to load a whole fhip if they would; and if they were, they would not chufe to venture their whole upon one bottom. In fhort, as the price of the freight is fixed, and is always the fame whether the articles are ready for embarkation or not, the planters wait till they are
preffed

pressed by the captains themselves to hasten the exportation. All these several reasons are the cause why vessels only of a moderate size are generally employed upon this service. The larger they would be, the longer time they would be detained in America.

Virginia always pays 1 *l.* 19 *s.* $4\frac{1}{2}d.$ freight for every barrel of tobacco, and Maryland ony 1 *l.* 14 *s.* $5\frac{1}{4}d.$ This difference is owing to the less value of the merchandise, and to the greater expedition made in loading it. The English merchant loses by the carriage, but it is made up to him by the commissions. As he is always employed in all the sales and purchases made for the colonists, he is amply compensated for his losses and his trouble, by an allowance of five *per cent.* upon these commissions.

This navigation employs two hundred and fifty ships, which make up 30,000 tons. They take in a hundred thousand barrels of tobacco from the two colonies, which, at the rate of eight hundred pounds a-barrel, make eighty millions of pounds weight. That part of the commodity which grows between York and James rivers, and in some other places, is extremely dear; but the whole taken upon an average sells only for about $2\frac{1}{4}d.$ a pound in England, which makes in all 738,281 *l.* 5 *s.* Besides the advantage it is of to Britain to exchange its manufactures to the amount of this sum, it gains another by the re-exportation of four fifths of the tobacco. This alone is an object of 442,968 *l*. 15 *s*. besides what is to be reckoned for freight and commission.

The custom-house duties are a still more considerable object to government. There is a tax of about $6\frac{1}{4}d$. upon every pound of tobacco that enters the kingdom. This, supposing the whole eighty millions of pounds imported to remain in it, would bring the state 2,078,124 *l*. 17 *s*. $9\frac{1}{4}d$. but as four fifths are re-exported, and all the duties are remitted upon that portion, the public revenue gains only 831,250 *l*. 10 *s*. $1\frac{1}{4}d$. Experience teaches, that a third of this must be deducted for prompt payment of what the merchant has a right to be eighteen months in paying, and to allow for the smuggling that is carried on in the small ports as well as in the large ones. This deduction will amount to 277,084 *l*. 2 *s*. $11\frac{1}{4}d$. and there will consequently remain for government no more than 554,168 *l*. 16 *s*. $4\frac{1}{2}d$.

Notwithstanding these last abuses, Virginia and Maryland are much more advantageous to Great Britain than the other northern colonies, more so even than Carolina.

CHAP.

CHAP. III.
Of CAROLINA.

1. *Origin.*

CAROLINA extends three hundred miles along the coast, which is two hundred miles broad, as far as the Apalachian mountains. It was discovered by the Spaniards, soon after the first expeditions in the new world; but as they found no gold there to satisfy their avarice, they despised it. Admiral Coligny, with more prudence and ability, opened an asylum there to the industry of the French protestants; but the fanaticism that pursued them soon destroyed all their hopes, which were totally lost in the murder of that just, humane, and enlightened man. Some English succeeded them towards the end of the 16th century; who, by an unaccountable caprice, were induced to abandon this fertile soil, in order to go and cultivate a more ungrateful land, and in a less agreeable climate.

2. *System of religious and civil government established by Locke.*

THERE was not a single European remaining in Carolina, when the lords Berkeley,

Clarendon, Albemarle, Craven, and Ashley, Sir George Carteret, Sir William Berkeley, and Sir William Colleton, obtained from Charles II. in 1663, a grant of that fine country. The plan of government for this new colony was laid down by the famous Locke. A philosopher who was a friend to mankind, and to that moderation and justice which ought to be the rule of their actions, could not find better means to oppose the prevalence of fanaticism, than by an unlimited toleration in matters of religion; but not daring openly to attack the prejudices of his time, which were as much the effect of the virtues as of the crimes of the age, he endeavoured at least to reconcile them, if possible, with a principle of reason and humanity. The wild inhabitants of America, said he, have no idea of a revelation; it would, therefore, be the height of extravagance to make them suffer for their ignorance. The different sects of Christians who might come to people the colony, would, without doubt, expect a liberty of conscience there, which priests and princes refused them in Europe; nor should Jews or Pagans be rejected on account of a blindness which lenity and persuasion might contribute to remove. Such was the reasoning of Mr Locke with men prejudiced and influenced by opinions which no one hitherto had taken the

liberty

liberty to call in queſtion. Diſguſted with the troubles and misfortunes which the different ſyſtems of religion had given birth to in Europe, they readily acquieſced in the arguments he propoſed to them. They admitted toleration in the ſame manner as intolerance is received, without examining into the merits of it. The only reſtriction laid upon this ſaving principle was, that every perſon, claiming the protection of that ſettlement, ſhould at the age of ſeventeen regiſter themſelves in ſome particular communion.

The Engliſh philoſopher was not ſo favourable to civil liberty. Whether it were, that thoſe who had fixed upon him to trace out a plan of government had reſtrained his views, as will be the caſe with every writer who employs his pen for great men or miniſters; or whether Locke, being more of a metaphyſician than a ſtateſman, purſued philoſophy only in thoſe tracts which had been opened by Deſcartes and Leibnitz; the ſame man, who had diſſipated and deſtroyed ſo many errors in his theory concerning the origin of ideas, made but very feeble and uncertain advances in the path of legiſlation. The author of a work, whoſe continuance will render the glory of the French nation immortal, even when tyranny ſhall have broken all the ſprings, and all the monuments of the genius and merit of a people esteemed by the whole world for so many amiable and brilliant qualities; even Montesquieu himself, did not perceive that he was making men for governments, instead of making governments for men.

The code of Carolina, by a singularity not to be accounted for in an Englishman and a philosopher, gave to the eight proprietors who founded the settlement, and to their heirs, not only all the rights of a monarch, but likewise all the powers of legislation.

The court, which was composed of this sovereign body, and was called the Palatine Court, was invested with the right of nominating to all employments and dignities, and even with that of conferring nobility, but under new and unprecedented titles. For instance, they were to create in each county two Caciques, each of whom was to be possessed of twenty-four thousand acres of land; and a Landgrave, who was to be possessed of fourscore thousand. The persons on whom these honours should be bestowed were to compose the upper house; and their possessions were made unalienable, a circumstance totally inconsistent with good policy. They had only the right of farming or letting out a third part of them at the most for the continuance of three lives.

The lower house was formed of the deputies from the several counties and towns. The

The number of this reprefentative body was to be increafed in proportion as the colony grew more populous. No tenant was to pay more than one fhilling per acre, and even this rent was redeemable. All the inhabitants, however, both flaves and freemen, were under an obligation to take arms upon the firft order they fhould receive from the Palatine Court.

It was not long before the faults of a conftitution, in which the powers of the ftate were fo unequally divided, began to difcover themfelves. The proprietary lords, influenced by defpotic principles, ufed every endeavour to eftablifh an arbitrary government. On the other hand, the colonifts, who were not ignorant of the general rights of mankind, exerted themfelves with equal zeal to avoid fervitude. From this ftruggle of oppofite interefts arofe an inevitable confufion, which put a ftop to every ufeful effort of induftry. The whole province, diftracted with quarrels, diffentions, and tumults, was rendered incapable of making any progrefs, whatever improvements had been expected from the peculiar advantages of its fituation.

Nor were thefe evils fufficient: new ones arofe, as if a remedy could only be attained from an excefs of grievances. Granville, who, as the oldeft of the proprietors, was in 1705 fole governor of the colony, formed
the

the resolution of obliging all the non-conformists, who made up two-thirds of the people, to embrace the forms of worship established in England. This act of violence, though disavowed and rejected by the mother country, inflamed the minds of the people. In 1720, while this animosity was still prevailing, the province was attacked by several bands of savages, driven to despair by a continued course of the most atrocious insolence and injustice. Those unfortunate wretches were all conquered, and all put to the sword: but the courage and vigour which this war revived in the breasts of the colonists was the prelude to the fall of their oppressors. Those tyrants having refused to contribute to the expences of an expedition, the immediate benefits of which they claimed to themselves, were all, excepting Carteret, who still preserved one eighth of the country, stripped in 1728 of their prerogatives, which they had only known how to make an ill use of. They received, however, 23,625 *l.* by way of compensation. From this time the crown resumed the government; and in order to give the colony a foretaste of its moderation, bestowed on it the same constitution as on others. It was further divided into two separate governments, under the names of North and South Carolina, in order to facilitate the administration of of it. It is from this happy period that the prosperity of this great province is to be dated.

3. *Climate and produce.*

THERE is not, perhaps, throughout the new world, a climate to be compared with that of Carolina. The two seasons of the year, which, for the most part, only moderate the excesses of the two others, are here delightful. The heats of the summer are not excessive; and the cold of the winter is only felt in the mornings and evenings. The fogs, which are always common upon a coast of any length, are dispersed before the middle of the day. But, on the other hand, here, as well as in every other part almost of America, the inhabitants are subject to such sudden and violent changes of weather, as oblige them to observe a regularity in their diet and clothing which would be unnecessary in a more settled climate. Another inconvenience, peculiar to this tract of the northern continent, is that of being tormented with hurricanes; but these are less frequent and less violent than in the islands.

A vast, melancholy, uniform, unvaried plain extends from the sea-shore fourscore or a hundred miles within land. From this distance the country, beginning to rise, affords

fords a more pleafing profpect, a purer and drier air. This part, before the arrival of the Englifh, was covered with one immenfe foreft, reaching as far as the Apalachian mountains. It confifted of large trees growing, as nature had caft them, without order or defign, at unequal diftances, and not encumbered with underwood; by which means more land could be cleared here in a week, than in feveral months among us.

The foil of Carolina is very various. On the coaft, and about the mouths of the rivers, which fall into the fea, it is either covered with impracticable and unhealthful moraffes; or made up of a pale, light, fandy earth, which produces nothing. In one part, it is barren to an extreme; in another, among the numberlefs ftreams that divide the country, it is exceffively fruitful. At a diftance from the coafts, there are found fometimes large waftes of white fand, which produce nothing but pines; at others there are lands, where the oak and the walnut-tree announce fertility. Thefe variations ceafe when you get into the inland parts, and the country every where is agreeable and rich.

Admirably adapted as thefe fpots are for the purpofes of cultivation, the province does not want others equally favourable for the breeding of cattle. Thoufands of horned cattle are raifed here; which go out in the morn-

morning, without a herdsman, to feed in the woods, and return home at night of their own accord. Their hogs, which are suffered to fatten themselves in the same manner, are still more numerous and much better in their kind. But mutton degenerates there both in flesh and wool. For this reason it is less common.

In 1723, the whole colony consisted of no more than four thousand white people, and thirty-two thousand blacks. Its exportations to other parts of America and to Europe did not exceed 216,562*l*. 10*s*. Since that time it hath acquired a degree of splendour which it owes entirely to the enjoyment of liberty.

South Carolina, though it hath succeeded in establishing a considerable barter trade with the savages, hath gained a manufacture of linens by means of the French refugees, and invented a new kind of stuff by mixing the silk it produces with its wool; yet is its progress principally to be attributed to the produce of rice and indigo.

The first of these articles was brought there by an accident. A ship, on its return from India, ran aground on this coast. It was laden with rice; which, being tossed on shore by the waves, grew up again. This unexpected good fortune led them to try the cultivation of a commodity which the soil seemed of itself to require. For a long time
little

little progress was made in it; because the colonists being obliged to send their crops to the mother country, from whence they were shipped again for Spain and Portugal, where the consumption was, sold them at so low a price that it scarce answered the expences of cultivation. Since 1730, when a more enlightened ministry gave them permission to export and sell their grain themselves at foreign markets, an increase of profit has produced an additional growth of the commodity. The quantity is at present greatly augmented, and may be still more; but whether so much to the benefit of the colony, is doubtful. Of all productions, rice is the most detrimental to the salubrity of the climate: at least, it hath been esteemed so in the Milanese, where the peasants on the rice-grounds are all of them sallow complectioned and dropsical; and in France, where that article hath been totally prohibited. Egypt had without doubt its precautions against the ill effects of a grain in other respects so nutritious. China must also have its preservatives, which art sets up against nature, whose favours are sometimes attended with pernicious consequences. Perhaps also under the torrid zone, where rice grows in the greatest abundance, the heat, which makes it flourish in the midst of water, quickly disperses the moist and noxious vapours

pours that exhale from the rice-fields. But if the cultivation of rice should one day come to be neglected in Carolina, that of indigo will make ample amends for it.

This plant, which is a native of Indostan, was first brought to perfection in Mexico and the Leeward islands. It was tried later, and with less success, in South Carolina. This principal ingredient in dying is there of so inferior a quality, that it is scarce sold at half the price it bears in other places. Yet those who cultivate it do not despair in time of supplanting both the Spaniards and French at every market. The goodness of their climate, the extent of their lands, the plenty and cheapness of their provisions, the opportunities they have of supplying themselves with utensils and of procuring slaves; every thing, in short, flatters their expectation: and the same hope has always extended itself to the inhabitants of North Carolina.

It is well known, that this country was the first, on the continent of the new world, on which the English landed; for here is the bay of Roanoak, which Raleigh took possession of in 1585. A total emigration, in a short time, left it destitute of colonists; nor did it begin to be repeopled, even when large settlements were established in the neighbouring countries. We cannot otherwise account for this dereliction, than from

the

the obstacles which trading vessels had to encounter in this beautiful region. None of its rivers are deep enough to admit ships of more than seventy or eighty tons. Those of greater burden are forced to anchor between the continent and some adjacent islands. The tenders, which are employed in lading and unlading them, augment the expence and trouble both of their exports and imports.

From this circumstance, probably, it was, that North-Carolina in the beginning was inhabited only by a set of wretches without name, laws, or profession. In proportion as the lands in the neighbouring colonies grew more scarce, those who were not able to purchase them betook themselves to a country where they could get lands without purchase. Refugees of other kinds availed themselves of the same resource. Order and property became established at the same time; and this colony, with fewer advantages than South-Carolina, obtained a greater number of European settlers.

The first people, whom chance dispersed along these savage coasts, confined themselves to the breeding of cattle, and cutting wood, which were taken off their hands by the merchants of New-England. In a short time they contrived to make the pine-tree produce them turpentine, tar, and pitch.

For the turpentine, they had nothing to do but to make to flits in the trunk of the tree, about a foot in length, at the bottom of which they placed veffels to receive it. When they wanted tar, they raifed a circular platform of potter's earth, on which they laid piles of pine-wood: to thefe they fet fire, and the refin diftilled from them into cafks placed underneath. The tar was converted into pitch, either in great iron pots, in which they boiled it; or in pits formed of potter's earth, into which it was poured while in a fluid ftate. This labour, however, was not fufficient for the maintenance of the inhabitants: they then proceeded to grow corn; and for a long time were contented with maize, as their neighbours in South-Carolina were obliged to be, where the wheat being fubject to mildew, and to exhauft itfelf in ftraw, never throve. But several experiments having proved to the North-Carolinians that they were not liable to the fame inconvenience, they fucceeded fo far in the cultivation of that grain, that they were even able to fupply a confiderable exportation. Rice and indigo have been but lately introduced into this province, to join the harvefts of Africa and Afia to thofe of Europe. The cultivation of them is but yet in its infancy.

There is fcarce one twentieth part of the

territory belonging to the two Carolinas that is cleared; and, at this time, the only cultivated spots are those which are the most sandy and the nearest to the sea. The reason why the colonists have not settled farther back in the country is, that of ten navigable rivers, there is not one that will admit shipping higher than sixty miles. This inconvenience is not to be remedied but by making roads or canals; and works of that kind require so many hands, and so much expence and knowledge, that the hopes of such an improvement are still very distant.

Neither of the colonies, however, have reason to complain of their lot. The imposts, which are all levied on the exportation and importation of merchandise, do not exceed 5,906 *l*. 5 *s*., The paper-currency of North Carolina does not amount to more than 49,118 *l*. 15 *s*. and that of South Carolina, which is infinitely more wealthy, is only 246,093 *l*. 15 *s*. Neither of them is in debt to the mother country; and this advantage, which is not common even in the English colonies, they derive from the great amount of their exportations to the neighbouring provinces, the Leeward islands, and to Europe.

In 1754, there were exported from South Carolina, seven hundred and fifty-nine barrels of turpentine, two thousand nine hundred

dred and forty-three of tar; five thousand eight hundred and sixty-nine of pitch or rosin; four hundred and sixteen barrels of beef; fifteen hundred and sixty of pork; sixteen thousand four hundred bushels of Indian corn, and nine thousand one hundred and sixty-two of peafe; four thousand one hundred and eighty tanned hides, and twelve hundred in the hair; one million one hundred and forty thousand planks, two hundred and six thousand joists, and three hundred and eighty-five thousand feet of timber; eight hundred and eighty-two hogsheads of wild deer-skins; one hundred and four thousand six hundred and eighty-two barrels of rice; two hundred and sixteen thousand nine hundred and eighty-four pounds of indigo.

In the same year North Carolina exported sixty-one thousand five hundred and twenty-eight barrels of tar, twelve thousand and fifty-five of pitch, and ten thousand four hundred and twenty-nine of turpentine; seven hundred and sixty-two thousand three hundred and thirty planks, and two thousand six hundred and forty-seven feet of timber; sixty-one thousand, five hundred bushels of wheat, and ten thousand of peafe; three thousand three hundred barrels of beef and pork; one hundred hogsheads of tobacco; ten thousand hundred-weight of
tanned

tanned hides, and thirty thousand skins of different kinds.

In the above account, there is not a single article that has not been considerably increased since that time. Several of them have been doubled; and the most valuable of all, the indigo, has increased to three times the quantity.

Some productions of North Carolina are exported to Europe and the Caribbees, tho' there is no staple town to receive them, and that Edinton, the ancient capital of the province, as well as that which has been built in lieu of it upon the river Neus, can scarce be considered as small villages. The largest and most valuable part of its exports is conveyed to CHARLES-TOWN, to increase the riches of South Carolina.

This town lies between the two navigable rivers, Cooper and Ashley; surrounded by the most beautiful plantations of the colony, of which it is the centre and the capital. It is well built, intersected with several agreeable streets, and its fortifications are tolerably regular. The large fortunes that have been made there from the accession and circulation of its trade, must necessarily have had some influence upon the manners of the people: of all the towns in North America, it is the one in which the conveniences of luxury are most to be met with. But the

dif-

disadvantage its road labours under, of not being able to admit of ships of above two hundred tons, will make it lose its present splendor. It will be deserted for *Port Royal*, which admits vessels of all kinds into its harbour, and in great numbers. A settlement has already been formed there, which is continually increasing, and may most probably meet with the greatest success. Besides the productions of North and South Carolina, that will naturally come to its market, it will also receive those of Georgia, a colony that has been lately established near it.

CHAP. IV.
Of GEORGIA.

1. *Foundation.*

CAROLINA and Spanish Florida are separated from each other by a great tract of land which extends one hundred and twenty miles upon the sea-coast, and three hundred miles from thence to the Apalachian mountains, and whose boundaries to the north and south are the rivers Savannah and Alatamaha. The English ministry had been long desirous of erecting a colony on this tract of country, that was considered as dependent upon Carolina. One of those instances

stances of benevolence, which liberty, the source of every patriotic virtue, renders more frequent in England than in any other country, served to determine the views of government with regard to this place. A rich and humane citizen, at his death, left the whole of his estate to set at liberty such insolvent debtors as were detained in prison by their creditors. Prudential reasons of policy concurred in the performance of this will dictated by humanity; and the government gave orders, that such unhappy prisoners, as were released, should be transplanted into that desert country, that was now intended to be peopled; it was named *Georgia*, in honour of the reigning sovereign.

This instance of respect, the more pleasing as it was not the effect of flattery, and the execution of a design of so much real advantage to the state, were entirely the work of the nation. The parliament added 9843 *l.* 15 *s.* to the estate left by the will of the citizen; and a voluntary subscription produced a much more considerable sum. General Oglethrope, a man who had distinguished himself in the house of commons by his taste for great designs, by his zeal for his country, and his passion for glory, was fixed upon to direct these public finances, and to carry into execution so excellent a project. Desirous of maintaining the reputation he had acquired,

quired, he chose to conduct himself the first colonists that were to be sent to Georgia; where he arrived in January 1733, and fixed his people on a spot at ten miles distance from the sea, in an agreeable and fertile plain on the banks of the Savannah. This rising settlement was called *Savannah* from the name of the river; and inconsiderable as it was in its infant state, was, however, to become the capital of a flourishing colony. It consisted at first of no more than one hundred persons; but, before the end of the year, the number was increased to 618, 127 of whom had emigrated at their own expence. Three hundred men and 113 women, 102 lads and 83 girls, formed the beginning of this new population and the hopes of a numerous posterity.

This settlement was increased in 1735 by the arrival of some Scotch highlanders. Their national courage induced them to accept an establishment offered them upon the borders of the Alatamaha, to defend the colony, if necessary, against the attacks of the neighbouring Spaniards. Here they built the towns of Darien and Frederica, and several of their countrymen came over to settle among them.

In the same year, a great number of protestants, driven out of Saltzburg by a fanatical priest, embarked for Georgia to enjoy peace and liberty of confcience. At firft they fettled on a fpot fituated juft above that of the infant colony; but they afterwards chofe to be at a greater diftance, and to go as far down as the mouth of the Savannah, where they built a town called *Ebenezer*.

Some Switzers followed the example of thefe wife Saltzburghers, though they had not, like them, been perfecuted. They alfo fettled on the banks of the Savannah; but at the diftance of four and thirty miles from the Germans. Their colony, confifting of a hundred habitations, was named *Purfburgh*, from Pury their founder, who, having been at the expence of their fettlement, was defervedly chofen their chief, in teftimony of their gratitude to him.

In thefe four or five colonies, fome men were found more inclined to trade than agriculture. Thefe, therefore, feparated from the reft in order to build the city Augufta, two hundred and thirty-fix miles diftant from the ocean. The goodnefs of the foil, though excellent in itfelf, was not the motive of their fixing upon this fituation; but the facility it afforded them of carrying on the peltry trade with the favages. Their project was fo fuccefsful, that, as early as the year 1739, fix hundred people were employed in this commerce. The fale of the fkins was with much greater facility carried on, from the

the circumstance of the Savannah admitting the largest ships to sail upon it as far as the walls of Augusta.

The mother country ought, one would imagine, to have formed great expectations from a colony, where she had sent near five thousand men, and laid out 64,968*l*. 15*s*. independent of the voluntary contributions that had been raised by zealous patriots. But to her great surprise, she received information in 1741, that there remained scarce a sixth part of that numerous colony sent to Georgia; who being now totally discouraged, seemed only desirous to fix in a more favourable situation. The reasons of these calamities were inquired into and discovered.

2. *Impediments that have prevented the progress of Georgia.*

This colony, even in its infancy, brought with it the seeds of its decay. The government, together with the property of Georgia, had been ceded to individuals. The example of Carolina ought to have prevented this imprudent scheme; but nations as well as individuals do not learn instruction from past misconduct. An enlightened government, tho' checked by the watchful eye of the people, is not always able to guard against every mis-

misuse of its confidence. The English ministry, though zealously attached to the common welfare, sacrificed the public interest to the rapacious views of interested individuals.

The first use that the proprietors of Georgia made of the unlimited power they were invested with, was to establish a system of legislation, that made them entirely masters not only of the police, justice, and finances of the country, but even of the lives and estates of its inhabitants. Every species of right was withdrawn from the people, who are the original possessors of them all. Obedience was required of the people, though contrary to their interest and knowledge; and it was considered here, as in other countries, as their duty and their fate.

As great inconveniences had been found to arise in other colonies from large possessions, it was thought proper in Georgia to allow each family only fifty acres of land; which they were not permitted to mortgage, or even to dispose of by will to their female issue. This last regulation of making only the male issue capable of inheritance, was soon abolished; but there still remained too many obstacles to excite a spirit of emulation. It seldom happens, that a man resolves to leave his country but upon the prospect of some great advantage that works strongly
upon

upon his imagination. Whatever limits are prescribed to his industry, are, therefore, so many checks which prevent him from engaging in any project. The boundaries assigned to every plantation must necessarily have produced this bad effect. Several other errors still affected the original plan of this colony, which prevented its increase.

The taxes imposed upon the most fertile of the British colonies, are very inconsiderable; and even these are not levied till the settlements have acquired some degree of vigour and prosperity. From its infant state, Georgia had been subjected to the fines of a feudal government, with which it had been as it were fettered. The revenues raised by this kind of service increased prodigiously, in proportion as the colony extended itself. The founders of it, blinded by a spirit of avidity, did not perceive, that the smallest duty imposed upon the trade of a populous and flourishing province, would much sooner enrich them than the largest fines laid upon a barren and uncultivated country.

To this species of oppression was added another; which, however incredible it may appear, might arise from a spirit of benevolence. The planters of Georgia were not allowed the use of slaves. Carolina and some other colonies having been established without their assistance, it was thought, that a country,

country, destined to be the bulwark of those American possessions, ought not to be peopled by a set of slaves, who could not be in the least interested in the defence of their oppressors. But it was not at the same time foreseen, that colonists, who were less favoured by the mother country than their neighbours who were situated in a country less susceptible of tillage and in a hotter climate, would want strength and spirit to undertake a cultivation that required greater encouragement.

The indolence which so many obstacles gave rise to, found a further excuse, in another prohibition that had been imposed. The disturbances produced by the use of spirituous liquors over all the continent of North America, induced the founders of Georgia to forbid the importation of rum. This prohibition, though well intended, deprived the colonists of the only liquor that could correct the bad qualities of the waters of the country, that were generally unwholesome; and of the only means they had to restore the waste of strength and spirits that must be the consequence of incessant labour. Besides this, it prevented their commerce with the Antilles; as they could not go thither to barter their wood, corn, and cattle, that ought to have been their most valuable commodities, in return for the rum of those islands.

The

The mother country at length perceived how much thefe defects in the political regulations and inftitutions had prevented the increafe of the colony, and freed them from the reftraints they had before been clogged with; and the government in Georgia was fettled upon the fame plan as that which had rendered Carolina fo flourifhing; and, inftead of being dependent on a few individuals, became one of the national poffeffions.

Though this colony has not fo extenfive a territory, fo temperate a climate, nor fo fertile a foil, as the neighbouring province; and though it can never be fo flourifhing as Carolina, notwithftanding it cultivates rice, indigo, and almoft all the fame productions; yet it will become advantageous to the mother country, when the apprehenfions arifing from the tyranny of its government, which have with reafon prevented people from fettling there, are removed. It will one day no longer be afferted, that Georgia is the leaft populous of all the Englifh colonies upon the continent, notwithftanding the fuccours government has fo amply beftowed upon it. All thefe advantages will fortunately be increafed by the acquifition of Florida; a province which from its vicinity muft neceffarily influence the profperity of Georgia, and which claims our attention for ftill more important reafons.

CHAP.

CHAP. V.
Of FLORIDA.

1. *History of Florida. Its cession from the Spaniards to the British.*

UNDER the name of Florida, the ambition of Spain comprehended all that tract of land in America which extends from Mexico to the most northern regions. But fortune, which sports with the vanity of nations, has long since confined this vague description to the peninsula formed by the sea on the channel of Bahama, between Georgia and Louisiana. The Spaniards, who had often satisfied themselves in preventing the population of a country they could not inhabit themselves, were desirous in 1565 of settling on this spot, after having driven the French from it, who had begun the year before to form a small establishment there.

The most easterly settlement in this colony was known by the name of St Mattheo. The conquerors would have abandoned it, notwithstanding it was situated on a navigable river at two leagues distance from the sea, in an agreeable and fertile soil, had they not discovered the Sassafras upon it.

This tree, a native of America, is better

in Florida than in any other part of that continent. It grows equally on the borders of the sea and upon the mountains; but always in a soil that is neither too dry, nor too damp. It is straight and lofty, like the fir-tree, without branches, and its top is formed somewhat in the shape of a cup. It is an ever-green, and its leaves resemble those of the laurel. Its flower, which is yellow, is taken as the mullein and tea in infusion. Its root, which is well known in trade, being very serviceable in medicine, ought to be spungy, light, of a greyish colour; of a sharp, sweetish, and aromatic taste; and should have the smell of the fennel and anise. These qualities give it the virtue of promoting perspiration, resolving thick and viscous humours, and relieving palsies and catarrhs. It was formerly much used in venereal complaints.

The first Spaniards who settled there, would probably have fallen a sacrifice to this last disorder, but for the assistance of this powerful remedy; they would, at least, not have recovered from those dangerous fevers they were generally subject to at St Mattheo, whether in consequence of the food of the country or the badness of the waters. But the savages taught them, that by drinking, in a morning fasting, and at their meals, water in which sassafras had been boiled, they might certainly depend upon a speedy recovery.

very. The experiment, upon trial, proved fuccefsful. But ftill the village never emerged from the obfcurity and diftrefs which were, undoubtedly, the natural and infurmountable confequences that attended the conquerors of the new world.

Another eftablifhment was formed upon the fame coaft, at fifteen leagues diftance from St Mattheo, known by the name of St Auguftine. The Englifh attacked it in 1747, but were obliged to give up their attempts. Some Scotch Highlanders, who were defirous of covering the retreat of the affailants, were repulfed and flain. A fergeant, who fought among the Spaniards, was fpared by the Indian favages, only that he might be referved to undergo thofe torments which they inflict upon their prifoners. This man, it is faid, on feeing the horrid tortures that awaited him, addreffed the blood-thirfty multitude in the following manner:

" Heroes and patriarchs of the weftern
" world, you were not the enemies I fought
" for; but you have at laft been the conquer-
" ors. The chance of war has thrown me in
" your power. Make what ufe you pleafe of
" the right of conqueft. This is a right I do
" not call in queftion. But as it is cuftom-
" ary in my country to offer a ranfom for
" one's life, liften to a propofal not unwor-
" thy your notice.

" Know

"Know then, valiant Americans, that in the country of which I am a native, there are some men who possess a superior knowledge of the secrets of nature. One of those sages, connected to me by the ties of kindred, imparted to me, when I became a soldier, a charm to make me invulnerable. You must have observed how I have escaped all your darts: without such a charm, would it have been possible for me to have survived all the mortal blows you have aimed at me? For I appeal to your own valour, to testify that mine has sufficiently exerted itself, and has not avoided any danger. Life is not so much the object of my request, as the glory of having communicated to you a secret of so much consequence to your safety, and of rendering the most valiant nation upon the earth, invincible. Suffer me only to have one of my hands at liberty, in order to perform the ceremonies of inchantment, of which I will now make trial on myself before you."

The Indians listened with eagerness to this discourse, which was flattering both to their warlike character and their turn for the marvellous. After a short consultation, they untied one of the prisoner's arms. The Highlander begged that they would put his broad sword into the hands of the most expert and stoutest among them; and at the same time

laying bare his neck, after having rubbed it, and muttering some words accompanied with magic signs, he cried aloud with a cheerful countenance: " Observe now, O valiant In-
" dians, an incontestable proof of my honesty.
" Thou warrior, who now holds my keen-
" cutting weapon, do thou now strike with
" all thy strength: far from being able to se-
" ver my head from my body, thou wilt not
" even wound the skin of my neck."

He had scarcely spoke these words, when the Indian, aiming the most violent blow, struck off the head of the sergeant to the distance of twenty feet. The savages, astonished, stood motionless, viewing the bloody corpse of the stranger, and then turning their eyes upon one another; as if to reproach each other with their blind credulity. But admiring the artifice the prisoner had made use of to avoid the torture by hastening his death, they bestowed on his body the funeral honours of their country. If this fact, the date of which is too recent to admit of credit, has not all the marks of authenticity it should have, it will only be one falsehood more to be added to the accounts of travellers.

The Spaniards, who in all their progress through America, were more employed in destroying the inhabitants than in constructing of buildings, had formed only those two
settle-

settlements we have taken notice of at the mouth of the channel of Bahama. At fourscore leagues distance from St Augustine, upon the entrance of the gulph of Mexico, they had raised that of St Mark, at the mouth of the river Apalache. But this situation, well adapted to maintain a communication between the two continents of the new world, had already lost all the little consequence it had at first obtained, when the English settled at Carolina in 1704, and entirely destroyed it.

At the distance of thirty leagues further, was another colony, known by the name of St Joseph, but of less consequence than that of St Mark. Situated on a flat coast, and exposed to every wind, and on a barren soil and an uncultivated country, it was the last place where one might expect to meet with inhabitants. But avarice being frequently a dupe to ignorance, some Spaniards settled there.

Those Spaniards who had formed an establishment at the bay of Pensacola upon the borders of Louisiana, were at least happier in their choice of situation. The soil was susceptible of culture; and there was a road which, had it been a little deeper at its entrance, might have been thought a good one, if the best ships that arrived there had not soon been worm-eaten.

These five colonies, scattered over a space

sufficient to have formed a great kingdom, did not contain more than three thousand inhabitants surpassing each other in sloth and poverty. They were all supported by the produce of their cattle. The hides they sold at the Havannah, and the provisions with which they served their garrison, whose pay amounted to 32,822 l. 10 s. enabled them to purchase cloths and whatever else their soil did not furnish them with. Notwithstanding the miserable state in which they had been left by the mother country, the greatest part of them chose to go to Cuba, when Florida was ceded to Britain by the treaty of 1763. This acquisition, therefore, was no more than a desart; yet still it was some advantage to have got rid of a number of lazy, indolent, and disaffected inhabitants.

Great Britain was pleased with the prospect of peopling a vast province, whose limits have been extended even to the Mississippi by the cession France has made of part of Louisiana. The better to fulfil her project, she has divided it into two governments, under the names of East and West Florida.

The British had long been desirous of establishing themselves in that part of the continent, in order to open a free communication with the wealthiest colonies of Spain. At first they had no other view but in the profits arising from a contraband trade. But an advan-

advantage so precarious and momentary, was not an object of sufficient importance, nor any way suitable to the ambition of a great power. Cultivation alone can render the conquests of an industrious people flourishing. Sensible of this, the British give every encouragement to promote culture in the finest part of their dominions. In one year, 1769, the parliament voted no less than 9,007*l.* 10*s.* 7½*d.* for the two Floridas. Here, at least, the mother for some time administers to her new-born children; whereas, in other nations, the government sucks and exhausts at the same time the milk of the mother country and the blood of the colonies.

2. *By what means Britain may render Florida useful to her.*

It is not easy to determine, to what degree of splendour this indulgence, with time and good management, may raise the Floridas. Appearances, however, are highly promising. The air is healthy, and the soil fit for every kind of grain. Their first trials of rice, cotton, and indigo, were attended with such success, that the number of colonists was greatly increased by it. They pour in from the neighbouring provinces, the mother country, and all the Protestant dominions in Europe. How greatly might this population be be increased, if the sovereigns of North America would depart from the maxims they have uniformly pursued, and would condescend to intermarriages with Indian families! And for what reason should this method of civilizing the savage tribes, which has been so successfully employed by the most enlightened politicians, be rejected by a free people, who from their principles must admit a greater equality than other nations? Would they then be still reduced to the cruel alternative of seeing their crops burned, and their labourers massacred, or of persecuting without intermission, and exterminating without pity, those wandering bands of natives? Surely a generous nation, which has made such great and such continued efforts to reign without a rival over this vast tract of the new world, should prefer to sanguinary and inglorious hostilities, a humane and infallible method of disarming the only enemy that remains to disturb her tranquillity!

The British flatter themselves, that without the assistance of these alliances they shall soon be freed from the little interruption that remains. It is the fate of savage nations, say they, to waste away in proportion as the people of civilized states come to settle among them. Unable to submit to the labour of cultivation, and failing of their usual subsistence from the chace, they are reduced to
the

the neceffity of abandoning all thofe tracts of land which induftry and activity have undertaken to clear. This is actually the cafe with all the natives bordering on the European fettlements. They keep daily retiring further into the woods; they fall back upon the Affenipouals and Hudfon's bay, where they muft neceffarily encroach upon each other, and in a fhort time muft perifh for want of fubfiftence.

But before this total deftruction is brought about, events of a very ferious nature may occur. We have not yet forgot the generous Pondiack. That formidable warrior had broken with the Britifh in 1762. Major Roberts, who was employed to reconcile him, fent him a prefent of brandy. Some Iroquois, who were ftanding round their chief, fhuddered at the fight of this liquor. Not doubting that it was poifoned, they infifted that he fhould not accept fo fufpicious a prefent. "How can it be," faid their leader, "that "a man, who knows my efteem for him, "and the fignal fervices I have done him, "fhould entertain a thought of taking away "my life?" Saying this, he received and drank the brandy with a confidence equal to that of the moft renowned hero of antiquity.

By many inftances of magnanimity fimilar to this, the eyes of the favage nations had all been fixed upon Pondiack. His defign was

to

to unite them in a body for the defence of their lands and independence. Several unfortunate circumstances concurred to defeat this grand project; but it may be refumed, and it is not impoffible but it may fucceed. Should this be the cafe, the Englifh will be under a neceffity of protecting their frontier againft an enemy, that hath none of thofe expences to fuftain, or evils to dread, which war brings with it among civilized nations; and will find the advantages they have promifed themfelves from conquefts made at the expence of fo much treafure and fo much blood, confiderably retarded, at leaft, if not entirely cut off.

END OF THE FIRST VOLUME.

www.ingramcontent.com/pod-product-compliance
Lightning Source LLC
Chambersburg PA
CBHW031749230426
43669CB00007B/547